GUIA

3D
3D

TRIDIME NSIONAL

DE

Buenos Aires

TRIDIMENSIONAL GUIDE OF
BUENOS

www.ba3d.com.ar

Publisher / Author:
Daniel Santoro
Luis Saenz Peña 235 1º piso.
Tel and fax: 4371-7690

Staff:
Design: Marcelo Rolla - Daniel Santoro.
Drawings: Daniel Santoro.
Maps: Zgroup s.a.
Photography: Otilio Moralejo and
Daniel Santoro. Colón Theatre
Photography by Raquel Bigio.
Texts: Daniel Santoro.
Texts corrections: Verónica
Bondorevsky.
Typing of texts: Silvia Susana Sánchez.
Translations: Liliana Capurro,
Lucila Lehmann
Assistants: Luciano, Francisco
and Sofia Santoro.
Distribution: María Pinto.
Thanks to: Carlos Copelo and Alicia
Monti, tango dancers, photography
models.

ISBN: 978-987-25590-0-7

Buenos Aires 2010

Declared of interest by
the Legislature of the
City of Buenos Aires.

Promoted by:
The Secretary of Tourism
from the Government of the
City of Buenos Aires.

Preprinted: ZGROUP sa
Uruguay 328 1º 1
Tel.: 4374-9229
e-mail: info@zgroupsa.com.ar

Santoro, Héctor Daniel
    Tridimensional guide of Buenos Aires. - 6a ed. -
Buenos Aires : B.A.3.D, 2009.
    160 p. : il. ; 23x16 cm.

    Traducido por: Liliana Capurro
    ISBN 978-987-25590-0-7

    1. Guía Turístca. I. Capurro, Liliana, trad. II. Título
    CDD 338.479 1

AIRES

Bicentenary Edition

Contents

Useful information **4**

History of the city of Buenos Aires **6**

Map of the city **12**

Tours around Buenos Aires **15**

Plaza de Mayo and surroundings **16**

Monserrat, Catedral al Sur **30**

San Telmo **36**

La Boca **44**

Puerto Madero **50**

Retiro and Plaza San Martín **56**

Retiro and Alvear Avenue **66**

Recoleta **70**

Palermo **82**

Palermo Chico **88**

Palermo Viejo / Las Cañitas **94**

Barrio Norte **98**

Corrientes Avenue **102**

Plaza Lavalle **108**

Plaza Congreso **116**

Belgrano **126**

Museum of Natural Sciences **130**

Abasto **134**

Tango and Folk **138**

Meat and mate **150**

Gastronomy and cultural guide **155**

Tourist Information Centers

Avenida Santa Fe 883
☎ 4312 2232 / 5550
0800 555 0016

**Ministro Pistarini
International Airport, Ezeiza**
☎ 4480 0224. Monday to
Friday from 10 AM to 5 PM

**Jorge Newbery Airport
Aerolineas Argentinas**
Central Hall
☎ 4771 0104 Monday to
Sunday from 10 AM to 5 PM

Florida
Florida 100
☎ 4313 0187 Monday to
Friday from 9 AM to 6 PM
Saturday from 10 AM to 4 PM

Puerto Madero
Alicia M. de Justo 200 - Dock 4
☎ 4313 0187
Monday to Sunday
from 10 AM to 5 PM
This Center also offers
information about Montevideo
City, Uruguay.

Recoleta
Quintana 596
☎ 4313 0187 Monday to
Sunday from 11 AM to 7 PM

Retiro
Av. Antártida Argentina
Bus Terminal, room 83
☎ 4313 0187 Monday to
Saturday from 7:30 AM to 1 PM

San Telmo
Defensa 1250
☎ 4313 0187 Saturday and
Sunday from 10 AM to 6 PM

$ **B**anks are open Monday through
Friday from 10 AM to 3 PM.
Shops are usually open from 9 AM
to 8 PM. Shopping malls are open
till 10 PM.

☎ **P**ublic telephones accept coins or
calling cards. Check the option on
the screen of the telephone before
using it. There are many Locutorios
to make phone calls around the city.

🍸 **T**ipping in restaurants and bars
usually amounts to 10 % of the
bill, though it will not be included
in it.

Taxis

They are black and yellow in color
and they are easily found on the city's
main streets. You may hail a taxi on
any corner but it is much safer to call
one on the phone through radiotaxi
services. The minimum fare is $ 4.60
and the passenger should pay the
amount on the fare meter. A trip
from the Center to La Boca should
not be more expensive than
$16.-. Tipping is
not required.

Public Holidays

January 1st
New Year
May 1st
Labor Day
May 25th
May Revolution
June 20th
Flag Day
July 9th
Independence Day
August 17th
**Anniversary of General
San Martin's death**
October 12th
Columbus Day
December 25th
Christmas

Buses

There are more than 150 bus lines in
the city and the buses are easily seen
on streets and avenues.
The minimum fare for a trip within
the city limits is $1.10 and the
maximum fare is $ 1.20. Buses are
furnished with automatic ticket
machines that only accept coins.

The legal currency in Argentina is called peso

100 pesos 50 pesos 20 pesos 10 pesos

5 pesos 2 pesos

1 peso | 50 cents | 25 cents | 10 cents | 5 cents

Five subway lines and one Pre-Metro line run across most tourist-attractive areas in the city and the service is quite good and inexpensive ($ 1.10 and 0.75). The fare is paid through tokens, which may be purchased in any station. The following are the names and areas covered by each line:

Ⓐ It runs under Av de Mayo and Av. Rivadavia. It goes from Plaza de Mayo to Primera Junta and it has a stop at Congress Square.

Ⓑ It runs under Av. Corrientes. It goes from Leandro N. Alem station (behind the Argentina Postal Service Building) to Chacarita station. It stops at the Abasto market (Carlos Gardel station).

Ⓒ It runs under Av. 9 de Julio and other streets. It goes from Constitución station to Retiro station. You may change in Diagonal Norte station for the rest of the lines. It has a stop at San Martín Square.

Ⓓ It goes from the Cathedral in Plaza de Mayo to José Hernández station in Barrancas de Belgrano quarter. On its way to Barrio Norte, it stops at Callao station, Agüero station, Facultad de Medicina station (under the Medicine College of the University of Buenos Aires) and Palermo station. After that, it runs under Cabildo Avenue.

Ⓔ It runs under Av. San Juan and it goes form Plaza de Mayo to Virreyes station, where you may change for the Pre-Metro line.

Ⓟ Pre-Metro: It goes form Virreyes station to a theme park called Parque de la Ciudad. The fare is $ 0.75 for those who take it on Virreyes station, but it is free for those who are changing from Line E.

Subway Lines

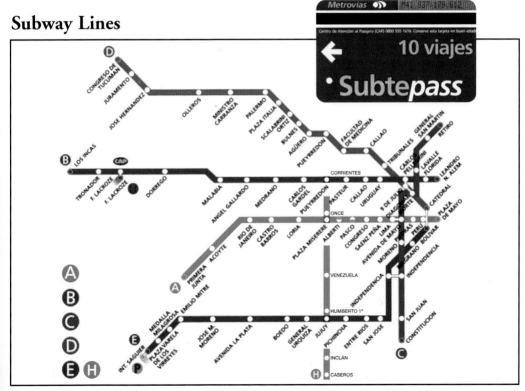

Brief history of the city of Buenos Aires

First foundation

When facing the need to stop the Portuguese forces' advance, Carlos I, king of Spain, sent commander Pedro de Mendoza to establish a stone fort somewhere in the Río de la Plata area. This fort would serve as the origin for a new city.

In 1536, Pedro de Mendoza arrived to the Rio de la Plata banks with around 2,000 men and he found the right place to build his fort on a high hill by the Riachuelo. He had some thatch-roofed mud huts constructed on a compact earth slope where we find Lezama Park today. In the beginning, good relationships with Native Americans allowed him to exchange low-value articles for food and other necessities. However, it was not long before this harmony came to an end and famine struck, which caused the population not only to decrease seriously due to confrontations but also to witness awful scenes of cannibalism.

This is a picture by Santiago Carbonell where we can see the scene of the foundation of Buenos Aires in front of the tree of justice, where Plaza de Mayo stands today.

Second foundation

In 1580, a new expedition departed from Paraguay. It was Juan de Garay who founded the base for the second time. He gave this settlement the name of "Ciudad de la Santísima Trinidad y Puerto de Santa María de los Buenos Ayres". The site he chose was two kilometres north of the first settlement. There he planted the tree of justice as a symbol for the generations to come.

As ordered under the Laws of the Indies, town planners used a checkerboard plan for the layout of the town. The plan featured a Plaza Mayor or central square, 15 blocks from North to South and 9 blocks from East to West. The only opening in the checkerboard was the Plaza Mayor (currently Plaza de Mayo), where enough space was left for a fortress. The city underwent the first change in 1594 when a stone wall was built for the fortress, which was only finished in 1713.

In the 17th Century, the city's population was 27,000 people. Increase in commercial activity together with smuggling and slaves commerce allowed the city to start expanding rapidly

Image of Buenos Aires in 1536 (First Foundation).

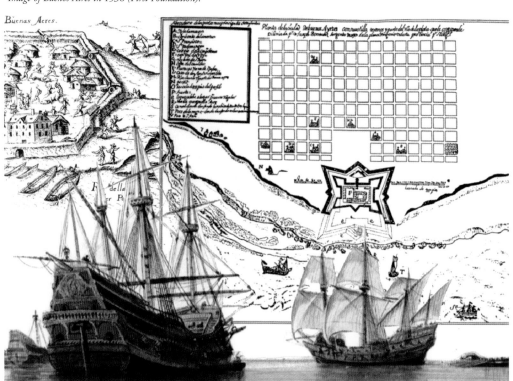

Tridimensional guide of Buenos Aires

British Invasions

In 1800, the British Empire started implementing its colonialist expansion policies. The second step in their plan, after winning the battle in Cabo de la Buena Esperanza, was undertaking the Río de la Plata area. In 1806, an English commander called Beresford disembarked with his troops in the south of the city. The first British invasion lasted 46 days and Liniers, from Montevideo, planned the recovery of the area. In 1807, another invasion took place and was repelled thanks to a heroic defense carried out by the local population, who later created the first group of Argentinian soldiers, called Patricios.

Independence

In 1810, after the Napoleonic War in Spain, a group of prominent citizens decided to request that the viceroy be dethroned and replaced by an autonomous governing group, the form of which was not still clear.
On July 9th, 1816, delegates from both the Capital City and the rest of the country proclaimed absolute independence from the king of Spain.

British troops surrendering to Santiago de Liniers in 1806.

Once Independence was proclaimed, a fratricidal struggle took place between the city of Buenos Aires and the rest of the provinces in order to determine the system of government for the new nation. In 1850, the nation started growing steadily due to the new political organization in the country. New quarters neighbourhoods called Constitución, La Boca and Retiro joined the urban checkerboard. To the west, the city expanded towards a town called Flores and, by 1880, the population had reached 300,000 inhabitants. Health and environmental conditions were not improved as the city grew. Between 1867 and 1871, 20,000 people died of cholera and yellow fever because there was no water system and garbage was thrown into the many creeks that ran across the city. When the cholera and yellow fever plagues hit Buenos Aires, the wealthiest families, who lived in the southern areas, were forced to move north.

View of Plaza de Mayo in the middle-18th Century. The main building is the fortress that stood where the Executive Office Building stands today.

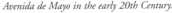

Inmigration

In 1880, during President Julio A. Roca's administration, the Federal Capital district of the Argentine Republic was established in the city of Buenos Aires. Torcuato de Alvear, mayor of the city in those times, decided that Buenos Aires should become the Paris of South America. He then had the Old Market (Vieja Recova) demolished, opened Av. De Mayo and developed a new urban area around Av Alvear and Barrio Norte. By 1914, and thanks to inmigrants, the city's population had grown eight-fold. The first signals of modern times started to appear in 1920, when the first skyscraper (Barolo building) was built and the first subway lines began working, but it was only in the 1950s that urban development made Buenos Aires one of the largest cities in the world. During the subsequent decades, the city took its current shape due to the growth of high-rise buildings. In the 1970´s, a highway network converging in the city's center was incorporated into Buenos Aires. The error in selection of the converging point caused serious traffic problems, which are accountable for high pollution rates in the downtown area. Nowadays, the city's population is 3 million inhabitants and the number of people living in the suburban area exceeds 9 million.

Avenida de Mayo in the early 20th Century.

View of the port in front of the Customs Building, 1859.

Architectural ornamentation of the city

The City of Buenos Aires includes a huge variety of architectural styles and its facades show rich ornamentations that transform this space in a unique place. If we pay attention to the buildings constructed from the end of the 19th century to the middle of the 20th we will see a vital world of atlantes, amorcillos, acanthus, volutes, fauns, Art Deco and Noveau details and infinity of eclecticism. This gives Buenos Aires city its personal enchantment and mystery. The tours may be started in Plaza Congreso, going through Av. De Mayo to Perú Street, taking Diagonal Norte and arriving to downtown streets, where you can see the bank's architecture.

Atlantes in Belgrano Avenue and Perú Street (1917)

Dante at the building of Unione e Benevolenza. ·treet and Rivarola Passage.

Bust of Leonardo at the building of Unione e Benevolenza. Peron Street and Rivarola Passage.

Dancing amorcillos at the monument of the Two Congresses.

High relief in bronze on the first floor of the old store Lutz Ferrando.

Clock with human figures in front of Plaza Congreso

Atlantes at Libertad Street on the corner of Libertad and Bartolomé Mitre Streets.

Art Deco low relief in the building of the Fraternidad. Hipólito Irigoyen and Combate de los Pozos Streets.

Spherical top part of the Confiteria La Ideal. Suipacha and Corrientes Streets.

Top part of stepped façade of the Opera Theatre. Corrientes and Suipacha Streets.

Barroc low balcony at the Actor's Association. Alsina Street and Entre Rios Avenue.

Corner with top piece of condors in the building at Belgrano Avenue and Peru Street.

Art Deco style in one of the buildings of the architect Kalnay. Avenue de Mayo and San Jose Street.

Renaissance columnata in the building of the architect Virginio Colombo. Sarmiento and Uruguay Streets

Ornamental pilastra in Cervantes Theatre.

Art Deco dome. Diagonal norte Avenue And Suipacha Street.

Balcony with expresionist details by the architect Colombo. Hipolito Irigoyen and Alberti streets.

Atlante in a low balcony on Palacio Pizurno.

Romantic relief on the building designed by architect Colombo. Hipolito Irigoyen Street.

Façade frieze on the top floor. Avenue De Mayo and Santiago del Estero Street.

Sculpture on the top part of cornise. Building La Inmobiliaria. Avenue De Mayo.

Atlantes on columns at the building located at Diagonal Norte and San Martin Streets.

Top part façade with sculptures on the building designed by architect Colombo. Hipólito Irigoyen Street.

Group of amorcillos on the low balcony on the building located in Saenz Peña and Alsina Streets.

Female figure dividing windows at on Palacio Pizurno.

Top part of cornices on the roof of the Congress.

Female bronze figures at the lateral entrance of the Congress.

Amorcillo on the low balcony of the building designed by the architect Colombo. Hipolito Irigoyen Street.

Art Nouveau iron and ceramics façade. Paraguay and Talcahuano Streets.

Dome at Galeria Guemes.

Map of the city with suggested tours

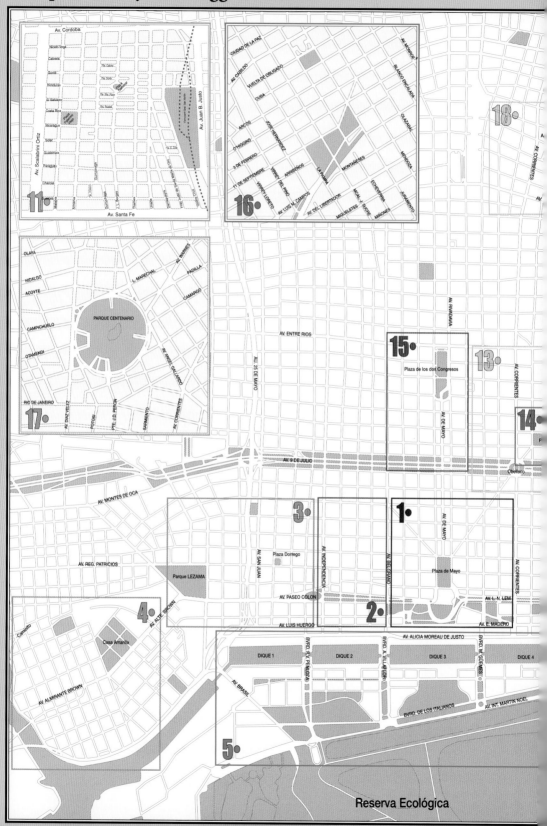

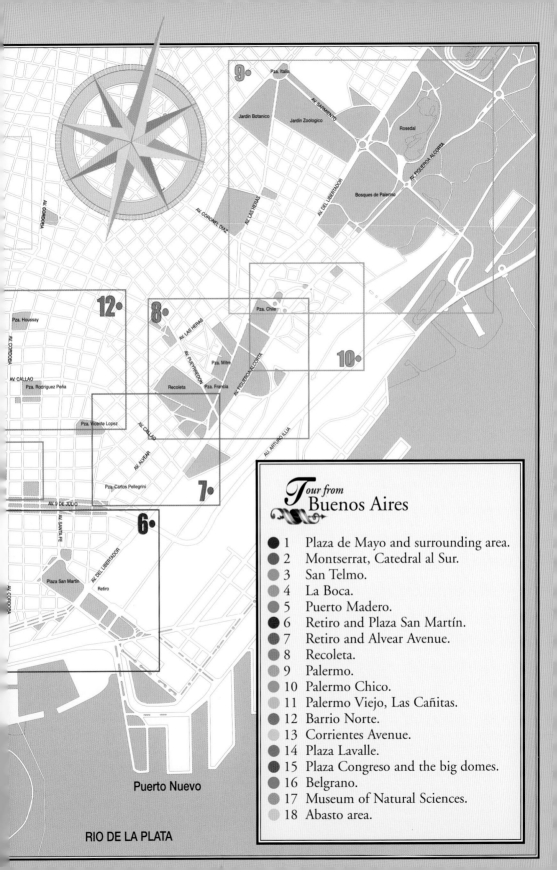

Tour from Buenos Aires

- 1 Plaza de Mayo and surrounding area.
- 2 Montserrat, Catedral al Sur.
- 3 San Telmo.
- 4 La Boca.
- 5 Puerto Madero.
- 6 Retiro and Plaza San Martín.
- 7 Retiro and Alvear Avenue.
- 8 Recoleta.
- 9 Palermo.
- 10 Palermo Chico.
- 11 Palermo Viejo, Las Cañitas.
- 12 Barrio Norte.
- 13 Corrientes Avenue.
- 14 Plaza Lavalle.
- 15 Plaza Congreso and the big domes.
- 16 Belgrano.
- 17 Museum of Natural Sciences.
- 18 Abasto area.

Puerto Nuevo

RIO DE LA PLATA

The purpose of this travel guide is to show you the most interesting parts of the city through a visual ride. Although Buenos Aires is an enormous capital, the 18 tours we suggest comprise each and every point of interest for those travellers who will spend just a few days in the Capital of Tango.

"The first impression when arriving in Buenos Aires is that of finding the last part of the world which can hold a big city.
In its condition as the last city on Earth, it ends up comprising any other city in the world and reminding us of them.
The second impression is that of the endless. An endlessly big geographical area which is reflected in what is endlessly urban about Buenos Aires..."

Franco Purini

Tour from Buenos Aires

- 1 Plaza de Mayo and surrounding area.
- 2 Montserrat, Catedral al Sur.
- 3 San Telmo.
- 4 La Boca.
- 5 Puerto Madero.
- 6 Retiro and Plaza San Martín.
- 7 Retiro and Alvear Avenue.
- 8 Recoleta.
- 9 Palermo.
- 10 Palermo Chico.
- 11 Palermo Viejo, Las Cañitas.
- 12 Barrio Norte.
- 13 Corrientes Avenue.
- 14 Plaza Lavalle.
- 15 Plaza Congreso and the big domes.
- 16 Belgrano.
- 17 Museum of Natural Sciences.
- 18 Abasto area.

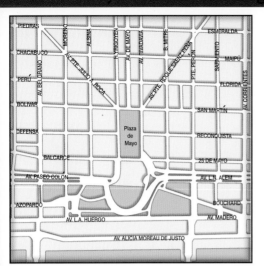

Eva and Juan Domingo Perón.

JUAN PERÓN   EVA PERÓN

FORJADORES DE LA NUEVA ARGENTINA

APARICIÓN CON V
Madres de Plaza de Ma

Mothers of Plaza de Mayo.

Plaza de Mayo is the original center of the city's historical area, which was founded by Juan de Garay in 1580.

Since 1810 it has been the scenary of every major political event in the country. In 1880, Juan Buschiazzo carried out an important remodelling of the square, in search of the classical symmetry that can still be recognized there. Some years later, French landscape designer Charles Thays gave the square its current looks. Its surrounding area grew when Av. de Mayo was opened, together with Diagonal Norte and Diagonal Sur streets, and when the City, as we call our downtown area, was developed.

Both in the square and it surrounding area, we can find architectural samples from different periods: the Cabildo, the Pyramid of May and the Cathedral date from the colonial period (18th Century and early 19th Century).

The Government House (Casa Rosada or Pink House) and the Municipal Building (former Hotel Victoria) date from the late-19th Century /early-20th Century period.

The Ministry of Economy (former Mortgage Bank) and the National Bank buildings belong to the monumental style developed by the government during the 1930s and the 1940s.

Plaza de Mayo was the place where Evita was acclaimed as a political figure and were the Peronist Party was born. In 1976, during the last coup in Argentina, the square became internationally known due to the presence of the Mothers of Plaza de Mayo, who would walk around the Pyramid every Thursday claiming for their "disappeared" sons and daughters.

In 1983, the square also witnessed the restoration of democracy.

We suggest sitting on one of the benches protected by trees to watch the intense activity in the City and enjoy the views, both of the Obelisco at the end of Diagonal Norte street and of the many belfries and domes along Avenida de Mayo.

Plaza de Mayo and surrounding area in 3d

Estatua ecuestre del Gral. Roca: *(Equestrian Statue of General Roca): He directed the conquest of the Patagonic desert, therefore integrating the whole territory of Argentina and exterminating many Native American tribes.*

Manzana de las Luces *(Square of lights). (see p. 25).*

Pirámide de Mayo *(Pyramid of May) (see p. 20).*

Museo de la Ciudad *(City Museum) (see p. 29).*

Museo Etnográfico Juan B. Ambrosetti. *(Ethnography Museum. Juan B. Ambrosetti). Moreno 350 (see p.29).*

San Francisco's Convent and Church. *The construction of the Convent started in 1587 and the Church's original building dates from 1754. In the church you may find a beautiful piece of tapestry by visual artist Horacio Butler. The current front of the building was designed in an eclectic style during the late 19th Century. The enormous dome is awesome and it can be seen from the corner of Moreno and Defensa streets. If you take a walk around the square, you will find a group of houses built during the same period. (see p. 24).*

Legislatura de la Ciudad *(Legislature of the City). (see p. 21).*

Diagonal Julio A. Roca

Chacabuco

Perú

Bolívar

Moreno

Defensa

Adolfo Alsina

Hipólito Yrigoyen

Balcarce

Paseo Colón

Ex Banco Hipotecario *(Former Mortgage Bank).*

Estatua ecuestre del Gral. Belgrano: *(Equestrian Statue of General Belgrano): It was formally unveiled in 1873 and it was created by French sculptor Albert.*

Museo histórico de la Casa Rosada. *(Historic Museum of the Government House). Hipólito Yrigoyen 219.* **Time Table:** *Monday to Friday, 10:00 to 18:00. Free entrance.*

Cabildo (see p. 18).

Casa de la Cultura (Cultural Center Former building "La Prensa" newspaper). (see p. 23).

Palacio del Gobierno de la Ciudad. (City's Executive Office Building).

Av. de Mayo

Maipú

Rivadavia

Perú

Diagonal Norte and Florida streets:
You may find huge domes and an interesting neocolonial building owned by the Bank of Boston with a shocking entrance door and hall in Plateresque style. If you walk down Florida street, you will get to Plaza San Martín and Retiro.

Diagonal R. Saenz Peña

Calle Florida

AV. DE MAYO

San Martín

Catedral Metropolitana
(Metropolitan cathedral): (see p.22).

Reconquista

Bme. Mitre

National Bank of Argentina. (Central House).
Typical sample of oficial architecture of the 30's century.

25 de Mayo

Leandro N. Alem

Government House
(Casa Rosada or Pink House):
It is built on the site chosen by Garay for the city's fortress in 1580. The building has undergone many changes. In 1882, two twin buildings were the seat of the Executive Office and they were later joined by means of an archway which is now the main entrance, looking on Plaza de Mayo. In 1873, President Sarmiento had it painted pink and it remained so until now.
(see p. 21).

Monument to Cristobal Colón.

The Cabildo

It was originally the seat of the city's government and its construction finished in 1764. At the back of the Cabildo there is a big patio where the jail for male prisoners used to be. When Av. De Mayo was opened, in 1889, a third of the original building was demolished and the same thing happened again when Diagonal Sur street was created.

The Cabildo was of great importance during the events that led to the proclamation of Independence from Spanish rule in 1810.

Its current appearance should be thanked to a detailed restoration work undertaken in 1939. In the patio behind the building, you will find a walkway that joins Hipólito Yrigoyen street with Av de Mayo. This is the ideal place to take a break and breathe the air of colonial Buenos Aires. Inside the Cabildo there is a small crafts fair and an inexpensive fast-food restaurant.

Night view of The Cabildo, behind the tower of The Legislature.

La Pirámide de Mayo
(*Pyramid of May*).
It was erected in 1811 to commemorate the events of May 1810. The original structure is still inside the current pyramid. It was created by Francisco Cañete.

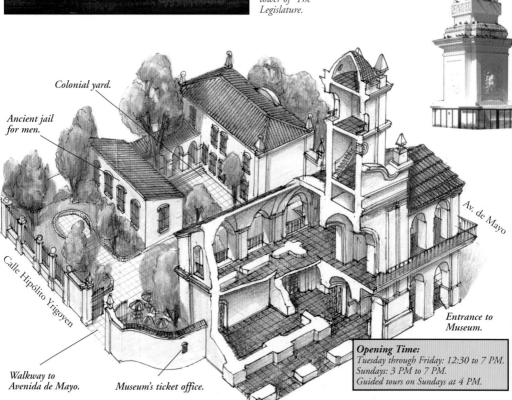

Colonial yard.

Ancient jail for men.

Calle Hipólito Yrigoyen

Av. de Mayo

Entrance to Museum.

Walkway to Avenida de Mayo.

Museum's ticket office.

Opening Time:
Tuesday through Friday: 12:30 to 7 P.M.
Sundays: 3 PM to 7 P.M.
Guided tours on Sundays at 4 P.M.

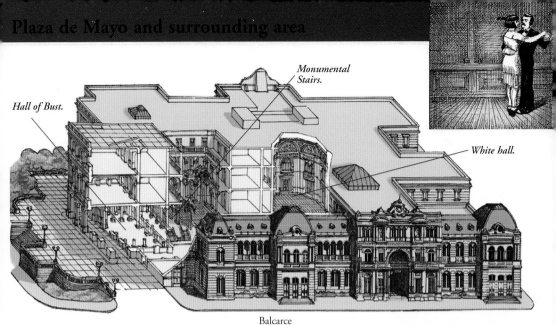

Hall of Bust.

Monumental Stairs.

White hall.

Balcarce

White hall.
View of white hall prepared for an official ceremony.

Executive Office Building
(Casa Rosada or Pink House).

It has been erected where the Royal Fortress of San Juan Baltasar de Austria, which was built in 1595, used to stand. The Fortress has been restored many times and partly demolished for the construction of the New Custom House. During President Samiento's government, the building was painted pink, thus establishing a tradition still in use and giving the building its popular name.

President Roca asked architect Enrique Aberg to build a new Executive Office Building. In 1894, the Italian architect Francisco Tamburini planned a new building, creating the complex monument that can be seen today. The result is an eclectic building, where elements of diverse origin, such as the French mansards and the loggias and windows by Nordic architects, coexist in Tamburini's characteristic classic language.

Panoramic view of the Palmeras Patio.

Lateral view of the Busts Hall in the ground floor.

21

The Cathedral

The original building dates from 1745 and the facade was modified in 1821 when a neoclassical gate was introduced according to the French trends of the time.

It was designated as Cathedral in 1836, once Joseph Dubourdieu had finished the magnificent new facade, which represents Jacob with his son, Joseph. (You may see it from the square across the street).

If you enter the building and walk along the nave to your right, when you get to the fourth column you will find a chapel containing the mausoleum of General San Martín. Soldiers of the Granaderos corps, a branch of the army created by General San Martín himself, permanently guarded the site.

Next to the first column on the right nave you may see a Russian icon, Our Lady of Vladimir, and also an image of Our Lady of the Forsaken, which was created in Seville during the 18th Century. Both the altar piece and the paintings in it date from the late 18th Century period.

The Monumental Colonnade: It faces Rivadavia street and it reminds us of the Madelaine Church or the Bourbon Palace in Paris.

Cathedral (inside view): The inside of the Cathedral was designed in a sober baroque style. In the picture you may see the rich ornaments in the altar, which was recently restored together with all the lateral chapels.

Guided tours: Monday through Friday at 1 PM. Saturdays at 11:30 AM. Sundays at 10 A.M. Meeting point: entrance to the nave on your right.

Icon of Our Lady of the Forsaken, late 18th Century.

Mausoleum of General San Martín.

Meeting point for guided tours.

General San Martín. He is the most important Argentinian hero. Liberator of the American continent, he is called "Father of the Nation".

Main altarpiece, 18th Century.

These twelve columns represent the Apostles.

Altarpiece of the Main Altar. Icon of the Immaculate Virgin. 18th Century.

Avenida de Mayo Between Perú Street and Plaza de Mayo

Former building of "La Prensa" (newspaper) and current House of Culture.

In 1910, after a visit to Buenos Aires, George Clemenceau said: "Undoubtedly, the most sumptuous building is that of the opulent La Prensa, which is known to be the main newspaper in South America".

In a prominently French style, you may see superb pieces of blacksmithing on gates and lamps. The inside of the entrance hall has recently been restored and it has recovered its famous original decoration, which is well worth a visit, as well as the Golden Hall on the first floor, where concerts and other cultural events are usually held.

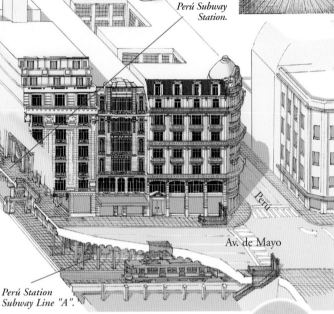

Roverano Passage connection with Perú Subway Station.

Av. de Mayo

Perú Station Subway Line "A".

Entrance door to the building of "La Prensa".

Perú Subway Station and Roverano Passage.

On the same side of the street as the building of La Prensa, you will find a subway station that belonged to the first subway line in Latin America. This station has been restored to its original condition by the City's Museum. A visit to Perú station will carry you to the Buenos Aires of the 1910s. If you walk across Avenida de Mayo from La Prensa building, you will see an interesting passage called Pasaje Roverano, which is connected with the subway station.

You may find the connection by entering the passage's ground floor (see picture).

Building on the corner of Perú Street and Avenida de Mayo.

Cortázar and "Los Premios".

On the corner of Perú street and Av de Mayo there stands a Liberty-style building that conveys a London-like atmosphere. The name of the cafetaria in the building is precisely London and it is an old and traditional shop, which has unfortunately been modernized. Part of the action in Julio Cortázar's novel "Los Premios" develops in this cafetaria.

Across Perú street, you may see a real display of luxurious buildings in a wide variety of Italian, French and Victorian styles. We suggest that you take a walk along Urquiza Anchorena´s Passage (on the odd-numbered sidewalk at 600). This passage joins Avenida de Mayo and Rivadavia street.

Julio Cortázar, , Argentinian Writer

Rivadavia

Avenida de Mayo

La Prensa Building. In this case, the sheltered central patio and the Golden Hall on the first floor facing Rivadavia street.

San Francisco Church and monastery.
San Roque Chapel.

It was started àt the beginning of the18th century and opened in 1752. In 1911 the altars were redesigned keeping original only the one on the right side. Most of the images and the pulpit are from the 18th century. The actual façade is also from 1911, according to the project of the architect Sackmann. We can see San Franciso de Asis, Giotto, Dante Alighieri and Cristhobal Colon. Behind the major altar we may observe a tapestry from the 20yh century made by Horacio Butler and opened in 1756 then restored after a fire in 1955, being most of his images from the 18th century and some from the 19th.

San Francisco small square

The location of this small square appears in the old maps of Buenos Aires as an open space. The statues that were originally around the Pyramid of May were installed in 1972 and they represent the Geography, Sailing, Astronomy and Industry.

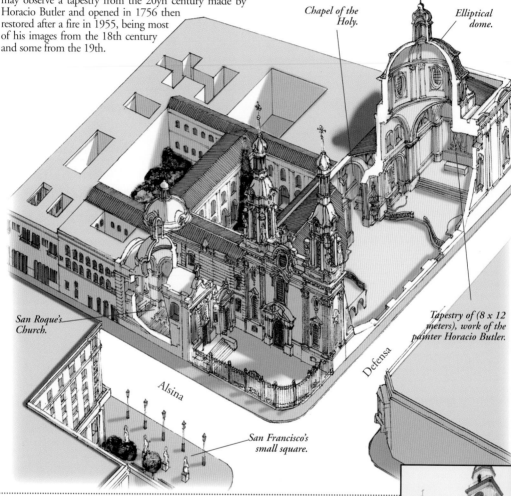

Chapel of the Holy.

Elliptical dome.

San Roque's Church.

Tapestry of (8 x 12 meters), work of the painter Horacio Butler.

Defensa

Alsina

San Francisco's small square.

Archways, patio and vault of Procuraduría de las Misiones.

Neoclassical façade, 19th Century. Entrance to the cloisters of the Procuratie of the Missions (Procuraduría de las Misiones).

Facade of San Ignacio's Church: It was built in 1675. Inside the church you may find many altarpieces and pieces of imagery that date from the colonial period. Pay special attention to the rose stained-glass window at the back of the church.

Manzana de las Luces *(Square of lights).*

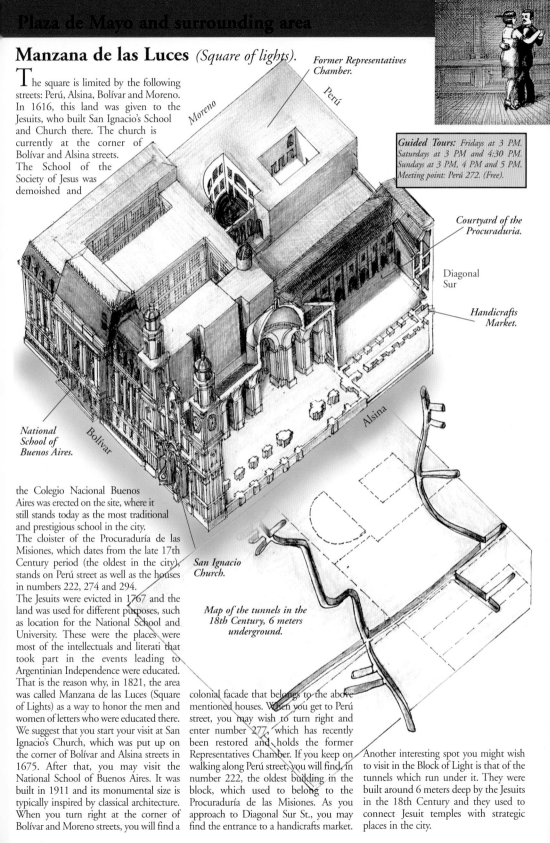

The square is limited by the following streets: Perú, Alsina, Bolívar and Moreno. In 1616, this land was given to the Jesuits, who built San Ignacio's School and Church there. The church is currently at the corner of Bolívar and Alsina streets. The School of the Society of Jesus was demoished and

Former Representatives Chamber.

Moreno

Perú

Courtyard of the Procuraduria.

Diagonal Sur

Handicrafts Market.

National School of Buenos Aires.

Bolívar

Alsina

San Ignacio Church.

Map of the tunnels in the 18th Century, 6 meters underground.

the Colegio Nacional Buenos Aires was erected on the site, where it still stands today as the most traditional and prestigious school in the city. The cloister of the Procuraduría de las Misiones, which dates from the late 17th Century period (the oldest in the city), stands on Perú street as well as the houses in numbers 222, 274 and 294. The Jesuits were evicted in 1767 and the land was used for different purposes, such as location for the National School and University. These were the places were most of the intellectuals and literati that took part in the events leading to Argentinian Independence were educated. That is the reason why, in 1821, the area was called Manzana de las Luces (Square of Lights) as a way to honor the men and women of letters who were educated there. We suggest that you start your visit at San Ignacio's Church, which was put up on the corner of Bolívar and Alsina streets in 1675. After that, you may visit the National School of Buenos Aires. It was built in 1911 and its monumental size is typically inspired by classical architecture. When you turn right at the corner of Bolívar and Moreno streets, you will find a colonial facade that belongs to the above mentioned houses. When you get to Perú street, you may wish to turn right and enter number 277, which has recently been restored and holds the former Representatives Chamber. If you keep on walking along Perú street, you will find, in number 222, the oldest building in the block, which used to belong to the Procuraduría de las Misiones. As you approach to Diagonal Sur St., you may find the entrance to a handicrafts market.

Another interesting spot you might wish to visit in the Block of Light is that of the tunnels which run under it. They were built around 6 meters deep by the Jesuits in the 18th Century and they used to connect Jesuit temples with strategic places in the city.

Legislature building of the City of Buenos Aires

This building was erected in 1930 by Architect Héctor Ayerza. It covers a big plot between Diagonal Sur street and Perú street and it is a sample of the eclectic trends in architecture during the first decades of this century. Its imposing neoclassical facade stretches along Diagonal Sur street and Perú street.

It has a very big and cozy library and there are also some halls designed for exhibitions on the ground floor. Halls San Martín and El Dorado, which have been recently restored, deserve a visit.

The tower is almost 90 meters high and on top of it there is a unique carillon for a clock that is still at work.

90 meters tower with carillon.

Representatives Chamber.

Entrance to Library.

Perú

Entrance to exhibition halls.

Main entrance to halls.

Diagonal Julio A. Roca

Main entrance.

Photo: Otilio Moralejo

Executive Office Building for the City of Buenos Aires.

It was built between 1891 and 1902 by engeneer Juan María Cagnoni based on the original proyect by architect Juan Antonio Buschiazzo. The building was enlarged between 1912 and 1914 without considering the original project.

The main entrance to the building is in Bolivar street.

At the entrance door, you will find the Flag Hall.

The plot where the Executive Office Building is located is considered a historic place.

Bolivar

Avenida de Mayo

Avenida de Mayo and its interesting spots

Along Av de Mayo you will find many stores that sell used books, you may purchase interesting pieces at a low price.

Pedemonti Restaurant in Avenida de Mayo 676, traditional quality food, quite expensive.

Café Tortoni.

B. de Yrigoyen

Av. 9 de Julio

C. Pellegrini

Tacuarí

Piedras

Legislature of the city of Buenos Aires.

Chacabuco

Hipólito Yrigoyen

Suipacha

Roverano Passage.

Cabildo.

Esmeralda

City hotel.

Perú

Av. de Mayo

San Miguel Palace.

Government House (Casa Rosada - Pink House).

Bolívar

Av. Julio A. Roca

Maipú

San Miguel Church.

Defensa

Roberto Arlt Square.

Roque Saenz Peña

Florida

Urquiza Anchorena Passage.

Hipólito Yrigoyen

Balcarce

Rivadavia

San Martín

London Bar.

Av. Paseo Colón

Reconquista

Former La Prensa Building, current House of Culture.

Executive Office Building for the City of Buenos Aires.

Plaza de Mayo.

Av. L. N. Alem

Tortoni Café, inside. It is always buzzing with activity and it has a Parisian atmosphere.

Front of Café Tortoni.

Café Tortoni

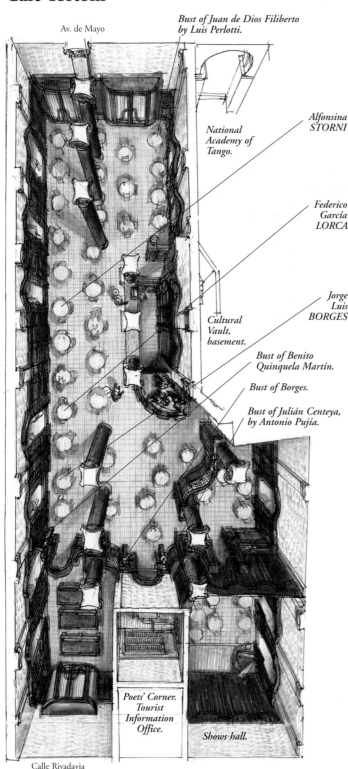

Av. de Mayo

Bust of Juan de Dios Filiberto by Luis Perlotti.

National Academy of Tango.

Alfonsina STORNI

Federico García LORCA

Jorge Luis BORGES

Cultural Vault, basement.

Bust of Benito Quinquela Martín.

Bust of Borges.

Bust of Julián Centeya, by Antonio Pujía.

Poets' Corner. Tourist Information Office.

Shows hall.

Calle Rivadavia

Our traditional Café Tortoni is located at the odd side of Av de Mayo between Tacuarí and Piedras streets. It was one of the first cafés in the city and it used to be the meeting point for inte llectuals and politicians. Nowadays, it serves as a real cultural center where jazz and tango events are usually held.

If you take a leisurely walk inside the café and pay attention to the walls, you may find several commemorative objects for famous personalities of the arts, which have been placed in the spots where those people used to sit. Thus, you will see them over the tables at which Jorge Luis Borges, painter Quinquela Martín, poet and journalist Roberto Arlt, Federico García Lorca, poet Alfonsina Storni and others used to sit.

In the basement of an adjoining building we find what we call La Bodega or The Vault, a kind of café where shows are staged and where you will have the opportunity to listen to some excellent tango music. The National Academy of Tango, the muse of which is poet Horacio Ferrer, is on the ground floor of the same building. You may enter through the door next to Tortoni Café. At the back of the café, there is a small library called El Rincón de los Poetas, or Poets' Corner, where the city government has installed a tourist information office.

The café has two entrance doors: one of the faces Av de Mayo and the other one, Rivadavia street. If you go out through the second door, you will find Roberto Arlt Square across the street. This is another oasis where you will be able to forget the buzzing of the city for a moment. Behind the "palos borrachos" trees and other species of indigenous vegetation, you will have the opportunity to admire a huge mural in relief by visual artist Alberto Cedrón. The apse you will see from the square belongs to San Miguel Arcángel Church.

City's Museum

On the corner of Defensa and Alsina streets there stands the City's Museum. The building is a good sample of how a bourgeois house looked like by the end of the 19th Century. The Museum serves an important purpose, since it keeps the urban memories of the city alive through several restoration and preservation activities (see Perú subway station). On the first floor, the Museum usually exhibits interesting pieces of its collection depicting uses and customs of the city's population. On the ground floor, a drugstore called La Estrella (The Star) has been preserved in its original condition, as it looked when it was the Old Pharmacy of the area. On the same sidewalk of Alsina street, next door to the Museum, you will find Puerto Rico cafeteria, a perfect spot to take a break.

Articles rescued from demolition sites by the Museum.

Household appliances from the Museum's collection. Inside view of the Museum.

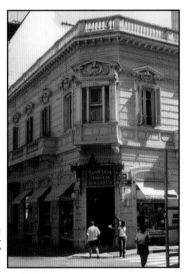

City's Museum on the corner of Alsina and Defensa streets.

Opening time: *Monday through Friday: 11 AM to 7 PM. Sundays: 3 PM to 7 PM.*

Etnographic Museum Juan B. Ambrosetti

Opening time: *Monday to Friday: 10 AM to 19 PM. (Free). Library consultant. Tel.: 4331-7788*

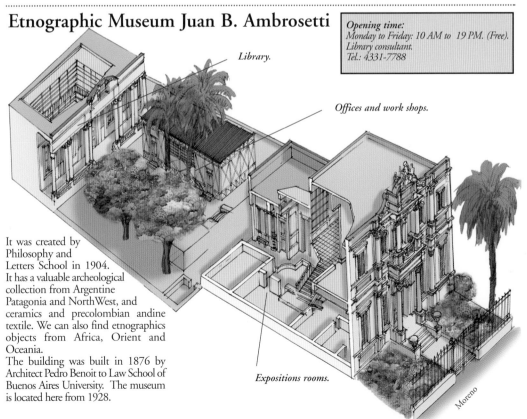

Library.

Offices and work shops.

It was created by Philosophy and Letters School in 1904. It has a valuable archeological collection from Argentine Patagonia and North West, and ceramics and precolombian andine textile. We can also find etnographics objects from Africa, Orient and Oceania.
The building was built in 1876 by Architect Pedro Benoit to Law School of Buenos Aires University. The museum is located here from 1928.

Expositions rooms.

Moreno

Monserrat, Catedral al Sur

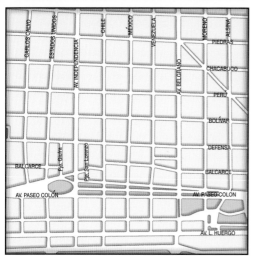

In the area bound by Plaza de Mayo and San Telmo neighborhood there are many places of interest as well as some streets and passages that stand out due to their shape. The block called Santo Domingo was the area where a crucial battle took place during the British Invasion (see p. 7).

If you walk along Balcarce street and cross Belgrano Avenue until you arrive at Independencia street, you will pass by some of the best places where you can enjoy tango shows, dance and have dinner. They all open in the evening. We suggest that you have a drink and relax in some of the bars at the corner of Chile and Balcarce streets, it will allow you to penetrate the quiet atmosphere of the city's southern neighborhoods.

Dancers Alicia Monti and Carlos Copello.

Catedral al Sur in 3 dimensions

Sample of fantastic architecture with esoteric symbols, near the corner of Bolívar and Chile streets.

Detail of the entrance gate.

Former National Library and current National Hall of Music: In this enormous neoclassical building, Borges worked as the director of the National Library for many years.

El zanjón de Granado. Old house from the 19th century beautifully recycled. It is located in front of San Lorenzo Passage. A place to be seen.

Typical house with balconies on the corner of Defensa and San Lorenzo streets. This area is crowded with artists' studios, making up the "Porteños" Montmartre.

When you walk along San Lorenzo passage, you will find a narrow house that is called the "tiny house". It is only 2.30 meters wide.

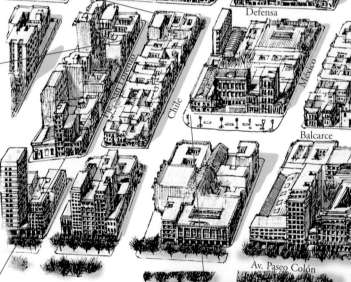

Perú

Estados Unidos

Av. Independencia

Bolívar

Defensa

México

Psje. San Lorenzo

Chile

Balcarce

Av. Paseo Colón

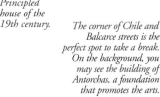

San Lorenzo's Passage : Principled house of the 19th century.

The corner of Chile and Balcarce streets is the perfect spot to take a break. On the background, you may see the building of Antorchas, a foundation that promotes the arts.

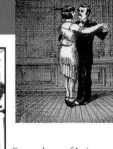

Martin Fierro: José Hernández (1834-1886), an Argentinian poet and journalist born in Buenos Aires, is the author of Martín Fierro, a folk epic poem that is considered a national classic in Argentina.

Former house of José Hernández and current building of the Argentine Writer's Association. Typical one-story house with a row of patios. It houses an important library and serves as location for several cultural activities.

Av. Belgrano

Venezuela

Moreno

Santo Domingo Church (see p. 35).

Piece of work by Alfredo Benavidez Bedoya, Argentinian engraver.

Museum of Engraving: *a large old house at Defensa 372 serves as seat for the Museum of Engraving. It has collections of Argentinian engravers from the 19th and 20th Century on display. The institution carries out an intense activity and it regularly organizes exhibitions.*

Opening time:
Monday through Saturday: 2 PM to 6 PM. Sundays: 12 to 6 PM.
Guided tours: *Sundays at 3 PM.*

We suggest that you walk by number 350 Defensa street, next to the Museum of Engraving. There stands the house of Bernardino Rivadavia, the first president of Argentina, in its original condition (18th Century).

General Belgrano, designer of the Argentinian flag. His tomb is in the atrium of Santo Domingo Church.

Balcarce Street

Walking through Balcarce Street you will arrive to Chile Street where you will find a great variety of bars, restaurants, discos and "tanguerías" with young people and tourists.

Frodo's: night bar and restaurant.

El Jimmy. night bar on Mexico Street.

Hostal de Granados. hostel, bar and restaurant.

Nanin. bar porteño.

Via via, hostel and restaurant on Chile Street.

La Raya. Restaurant.

Balcarce street seen from Avenida Belgrano and Chile Street.

Taconeando. Tango.

Molière. Café, restaurant, bar and tangos

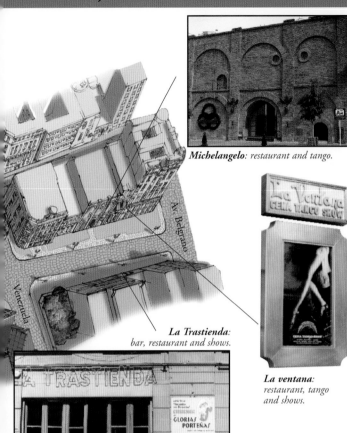

Michelangelo: *restaurant and tango.*

La Trastienda: *bar, restaurant and shows.*

La ventana: *restaurant, tango and shows.*

Our lady of Rosario Basilic Santo Domingo Convent

Belgrano Avenida and Defensa street. Its construction began in 1751 under the direction of Architect Antonio Masella. One of the towers was inaugurated at the end of XVIII century and the other one at the middle of last century. The inside lost its colonial style and the marble added at the beginning of the 20th century. It keeps English flags, taken during English Invasions when they occupied the church and the flags from the royalists that Belgrano donated to the Virgin.

Mausoleum of Gral Belgrano is located from the beginning of this century, in the atrium of the church. This is a work of Italian sculptor Ettore Ximenes.

On the tower, people can see replicas of the shots in 1807, because it has been reconstructed.

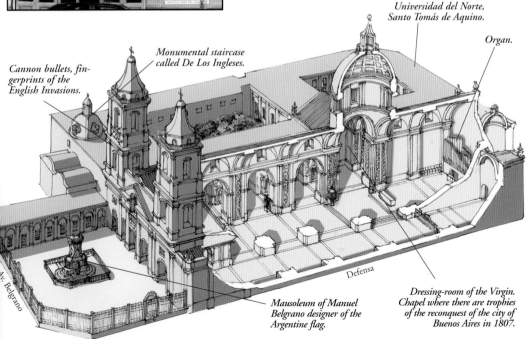

Cannon bullets, fingerprints of the English Invasions.

Monumental staircase called De Los Ingleses.

Universidad del Norte, Santo Tomás de Aquino.

Organ.

Defensa

Mausoleum of Manuel Belgrano designer of the Argentine flag.

Dressing-room of the Virgin. Chapel where there are trophies of the reconquest of the city of Buenos Aires in 1807.

Av. Belgrano

35

San Telmo

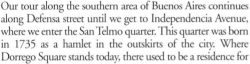

Our tour along the southern area of Buenos Aires continues along Defensa street until we get to Independencia Avenue, where we enter the San Telmo quarter. This quarter was born in 1735 as a hamlet in the outskirts of the city. Where Dorrego Square stands today, there used to be a residence for the Bethlehemite monks, south of the Lezama ranch (today, Museum of History and park).

The quarter's population was made up of aristocratic families until 1870, when they moved to the northern area of the city escaping the plagues partly caused by the poor health conditions in Buenos Aires. San Telmo then became a residential neighborhood and, in time, the large houses started to serve as tenement houses or conventillos where immigrants used to rent rooms, which led to growing deterioration of the buildings during the first half of the 20th Century.

It was only in the 1970s that some rules were established in order to preserve the quarter's buildings, thus keeping valuable pieces of architecture from damage. Nowadays, the area is plenty of antique shops, especially along Defensa street, between Independencia and San Juan avenues. This is the perfect place for a walk on Sundays, since there is an antiques fair in Dorrego Square (on Defensa and Carlos Calvo streets) every Sunday morning, opening at 10 AM. (see p. 41).

San Telmo in 3 dimensions

Lezama Park

It is the highest area along the riverbanks. During the 17th Century, it was used as an area for warehouses and slave cabins. It later became the ranch of the Lezama family and, in 1884, the whole plot was purchased by the city's government and used to build the park we can visit nowadays. It was restored recently and it has a sculpture garden and a watchtower.

Bar Británico *(Britanic bar)*

It is a mythical spot of Buenos Aires, crowded by artists and bohemians, the perfect place for the sleepless, since it is always open. Right across the street you will find Hipopótamus Bar, which is quite similar to the British Bar.

Russian Orthodox Church

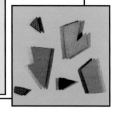

In front of the park you may see the Russian Orthodox Church, an exotic building with five onion-shaped domes erected in the early-20th Century period.

National History Museum (see p. 42).

Bolívar

Av. Caseros

Defensa

Av. Juan de Garay

Cochabamba

Au 25 de Mayo

Brasil

Balcarce

Av. Paseo Colón

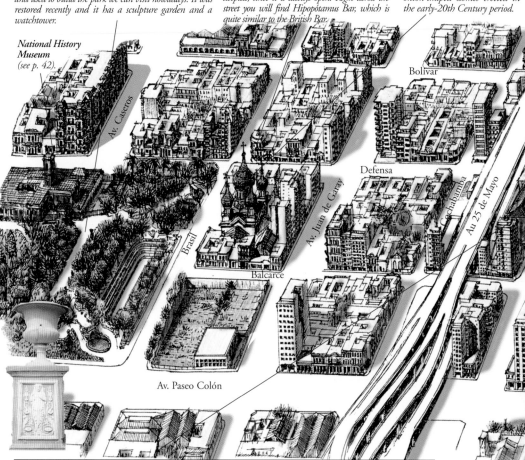

Museum of Modern Art: San Juan 350.
It houses important painting and sculpture collections of contemporary art, both from Argentina and from abroad. Exhibitions are regularly organized in the Museum. It had many famous directors, it was founded by Rafael Squirru and it gained dynamism and prestige during Raúl Santana's administration, a period during which great exhibitions were held, such as that of the Cobra group. The building used to be a tobacco storehouse and it was restored to serve as a museum.

Opening time:
Monday through Friday from 10 AM to 8 PM. Saturdays, Sundays and Public Holidays from 11 AM to 8 PM.
Guided tours:
for the public in general, Tuesday through Sunday at 5 PM; for institutions: request in advance by phone. Ticket price: $ 3. Wednesdays free in both wings.

Work by Raúl Lozza, Museum's collection.

San Telmo

San Telmo's Fair

It is held every Sunday from 10 Am to 6 Pm in Dorrego Square and adjoining streets. You may go and purchase antiques or small works of art, or you may just mingle with people and be entertained by street performers and tango dancers.

Forner-Bigatti Foundation

Facing Dorrego Square there is a house that dates from the 1930s, an example of rationalist architecture. It was the place of abode of Raquel Forner and Alfredo Bigatti, two well-known visual artists from Argentina.

Bar Dorrego

Humberto Primo and Defensa street. It is the most traditional and well-known bar in the area. Inside of the bar you may breathe the atmosphere of a typical tavern of the 1920's.

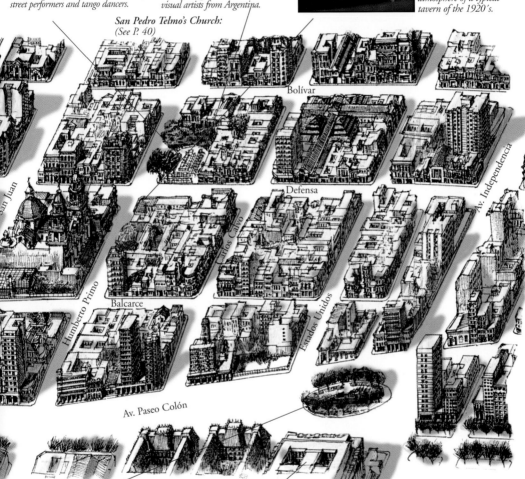

San Pedro Telmo's Church:
(See P. 40)

Bolívar

San Juan

Defensa

Carlos Calvo

Av. Independencia

Humberto Primo

Balcarce

Estados Unidos

Av. Paseo Colón

"El canto al trabajo" (Song for Labor), sculpture by Rogelio Yrurtia. The author was one of Rodin's disciples and he is known as one of the most important Latin American sculptors. (The work may be seen in the piazza located at the corner of Paseo Colón and Independencia Avenue).

Former Eva Perón Foundation and current College of Engineering

This building was designed during a military government in the 1930s and it is a typical example of German neoclassical architecture. It was built in the 1940s and it served as the seat of Eva Perón Foundation, the purpose of which was to aid the poor.

Ezeiza's Passage

It was built around 1880 and it has a row of several patios. This kind of buildings were called "casa chorizo" (sausage houses) in Buenos Aires and they were an Argentinian version of the old Roman Domus as adapted to plots of land that were just 11 meters wide. It also served as a typical tenement house that could hold a maximum of 32 families. It was restored in 1982 and it became a commercial passage. Today, you may find antique shops and souvenir stores that sell posters and cards.

Courtyard of the cistern.

Courtyard of the Tree.

María de San Telmo: store that sells articles for tourists, such as travel guides, posters, cards and souvenirs.

Courtyard of the Time.

Church of our Lady of Belén & San Pedro González Telmo

On Humberto Iº St. 340.

The construction of the church began in 1734 on the project plan by the jesuit architect brother Andrés Blanqui and the support of the brothers Juan Bautista Prímoli and José Schmidt and who finished the construction was the Italian master Antonio Masella; the last restoration was made by architect Pelayo Sáinz in 1918. The front was made in eclectic style, with some architectonic elements of Neo Colonial and Barroc styles and in the upper part St. Peter Gonzalez Telmo's image has been located. It has been recognized as National Historical Monument.

San Pedro Telmo's Church.

Dome of plant of eight side.

Jesuit Oratory.

Dome with coating of Stone.

Humberto Primo

Porch and facade neoclasic, ended in 1942.

Access to the penitentiary museum.

Courtyard of the 18th century.

Argentine Penitentiary Museum "Antonio Ballvé"

Humberto Iº 378 St. The museum is a 1760 building and the plans were made by the architect Antonio Masella. At the first time, it had been the Spiritual Retreat House for men. In 1767, when Jesuit Order was sent off, City Hall established here Women Jail under the supervision of Penitentiary Service until 1978 when the jail was moved to the neighborhood of Ezeiza. The Our Lady of Carmen Chapel, an 1734 construction, is located inside this museum.

San Telmo

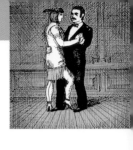

Dorrego Square in 3 dimensions

Dorrego Square.
Between Humberto I, Defensa, Anselmo Aieta and Bethlem Streets.
It was declared of National Historical Interest because this is where the people met to reconfirm their Declaration of Independence from Spain on July 9th 1816. Dorrego is the oldest square in the city after Plaza de Mayo Sq. On Sundays from 10.00 to 17.00 hs. an Antique Market functions here organized by City Museum, while the Square seems to go back into the past and dancers move to the sound of Tangos and Milongas.

Foundation Forner Bigati. Raquel Forner and Alfredo Bigati were two great Argentine artists. This house was their shop.

Antique shop from the 19th century specialized in phonographs and old record players on the corner of Bethlen and Defensa streets.

Bethlem

Anselmo Aieta

Defensa

Humberto Primo

Dorrego Bar, on the corner of Defensa and Carlos Calvo streets.

Housing building accomplished by the architects Poblet and Ortuzar of academic style, about 1920s.

Street performers and tango dancers on the corner of Defensa and Carlos Calvo streets.

Lezama Park

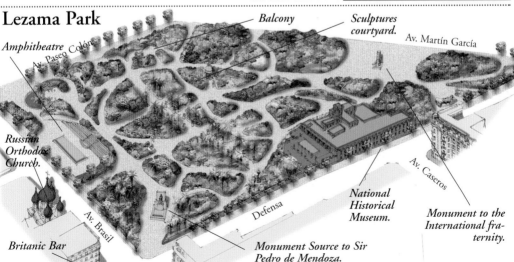

Balcony

Sculptures courtyard.

Amphitheatre

Av. Paseo Colón

Av. Martín García

Russian Orthodox Church.

Av. Caseros

Defensa

National Historical Museum.

Monument to the International fraternity.

Av. Brasil

Britanic Bar

Monument Source to Sir Pedro de Mendoza.

National Museum of History

The national Museum of History building used to be the house of the Lezama family. Its appearance is similar to that of an Italian palazzo, with a square-shaped tower that dominated the southern area of the city for many years.

Its 32 rooms made up one of the most important residences during the first half of the 19th Century. In 1897, the building was assigned to the National Museum of History, founded by Adolfo Carranza. The Museum's collection shows us a panoramic view of the history of Argentina since the 16th Century until the end of the 19th Century.

A special room devoted to General San Martín houses a reproduction of his room in Grand Bourg, France. Relics from the Jesuits' missions and trophies from the battle of Suipacha are also on display. The Museum has an important collection of drawings and paintings by travelling artists of the 19th Century, such as French painter Palliere, Italian artist Pellegrini and French engraver Gericault. Undoubtedly, the main work of art in this collection is a series of paintings on the War of Paraguay by Cándido López.

Entrance gate with archways in typical Italian style.

In the Museum's garden, a collection of cannons and bells from different periods.

Five domes carried in metal.

Crossings watching to the East held with chains.

Icon of the Santísima Trinidad.

Pulpits.

Choir.

Access staircase to the Shrine that this in the first floor.

Altar watching to the East.

Av. Brasil

Opening times:
Tuesday through Friday, from 2 PM to 6 PM. Saturdays and Sundays from 3 PM to 7 PM. Admission: free.

Russian Orthodox Church of the Holy Trinity

Brasil 315 St. between Defensa and Paseo Colón Streets.

This church was opened in 1904; the original project was made by the architect of Russian Holy Synod, Mihail Preobrazensky, and was adapted by the architect Alejandro Christophersen. The temple was built in Muscovite style of XVII century.

San Telmo

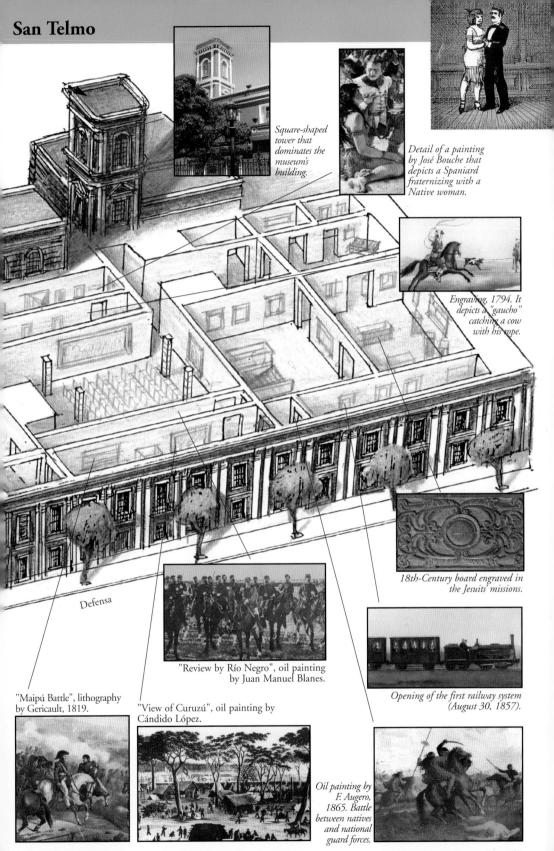

Square-shaped tower that dominates the museum's building.

Detail of a painting by José Bouche that depicts a Spaniard fraternizing with a Native woman.

Engraving, 1794. It depicts a "gaucho" catching a cow with his rope.

18th-Century board engraved in the Jesuits' missions.

Defensa

"Review by Río Negro", oil painting by Juan Manuel Blanes.

Opening of the first railway system (August 30, 1857).

"Maipú Battle", lithography by Gericault, 1819.

"View of Curuzú", oil painting by Cándido López.

Oil painting by F. Augero, 1865. Battle between natives and national guard forces.

La Boca

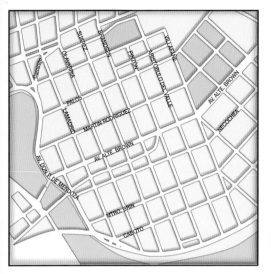

The origin of this quarter is undoubtedly connected with the "Riachuelo", on the banks of which it started to develop. The activity brought about by the river, the increase in trade, the presence of shipyards and other factors attracted people who settled down in this area of the city. It was not long before emigrants started to move into the quarter. Most of them came from Genoa, in Italy, and therefore, by 1870, la Boca had already acquired its own shape. It still remains as the only part of the city that has a close relationship with the river. The heart of the quarter is Caminito street, a narrow pedestrian passage almost 100 meters long which was built on an old stretch for rails and took its name from a famous tango song by Juan de Dios Filiberto. The typical houses in this area are made up of formed sheet metal and most of them have become either tenement houses or painters' studios. Their characteristic colorful walls arise from a project designed by painter Benito Quinquela Martín, who thought that painting the walls in different colors would give Caminito a definite character. If you walk along the riachuelo's bank, you will come across Nicolás Avellaneda bridge, which offers a full panoramic view of the area and the river. Next to this bridge stands the old transporter bridge, which was built in 1908 and is currently abandoned.

Caminito Street

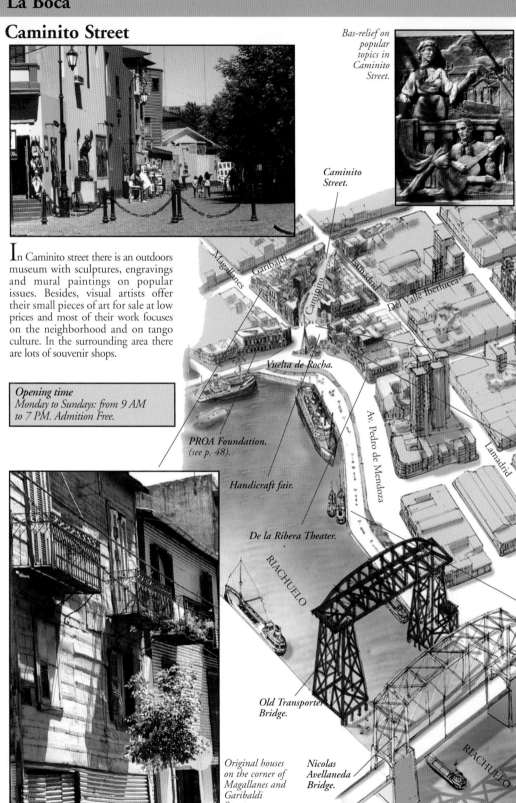

Bas-relief on popular topics in Caminito Street.

In Caminito street there is an outdoors museum with sculptures, engravings and mural paintings on popular issues. Besides, visual artists offer their small pieces of art for sale at low prices and most of their work focuses on the neighborhood and on tango culture. In the surrounding area there are lots of souvenir shops.

Opening time
Monday to Sundays: from 9 AM to 7 PM. Admition Free.

Caminito Street.

Magallanes

Garibaldi

Lamadrid

Camiñito

Del Valle Iberlucea

Vuelta de Rocha.

Av. Pedro de Mendoza

Lamadrid

PROA Foundation.
(see p. 48).

Handicraft fair.

De la Ribera Theater.

RIACHUELO

Old Transporter Bridge.

Original houses on the corner of Magallanes and Garibaldi Streets.

Nicolas Avellaneda Bridge.

RIACHUELO

La Boca

Museum of the
Boca's Juniors
Fans. *Includes
guided tour to
the stadium.*

Boca Juniors
Stadium.

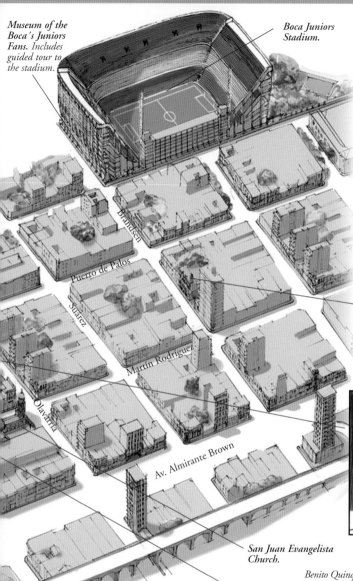

Brandsen

Puerto de Palos

Suárez

Martín Rodríguez

Olavarría

Av. Almirante Brown

*La Perla Bar, traditional place in the
city, on the corner of Pedro de Mendoza
and Del Valle Ibarlucea Streets.*

Voluntary Firemens
quarter.

*In the entrance to Caminito street,
you will find street performers and
many couples of tango dancers.*

San Juan Evangelista
Church.

*Benito Quinquela Martín School and Museum, located at
Pedro de Mendoza 1835.* (see p. 49).

*Old barges and tugboats remain stranded in
Vuelta de Rocha, which used to be a dynamic
commercial port in front of Caminito.*

Boca Juniors Football Stadium

La Boca neighborhood is closely related to the history of Boca Juniors Soccer Club, the most popular one in the city. Due to its vertical structure that seems to go beyond the sidewalk's limits, the stadium is called "La Bombonera". It can hold more than 50,000 spectators. Near the stadium, on the corner of Brandsen and Del Valle Iberlucea streets,

there are two well-known, excellent restaurants: la Cancha and El Carlitos. Further away from the stadium, in number 64 of Cafarena street, you will find another restaurant called El Obrero.

The area that stretches along Necochea

street between Brandsen and Olavarría streets is crowded with canteens that buzz with activity in the evening.

Proa Foundation

It organizes many cultural activities. Its rooms have served as exhibition halls for paintings of major local and international artists, such as German painter and photographer Anselm Kiefer, and Mexican painter Julio Galán.

"Mientras me despierto" ("While I Wake Up"), oil painting by Julio Galán.

La Boca

Quinquela Martín School and Museum

On the higher floors of Quinquela Martín Elementary School you will find the Museum of Painting and Sculpture. Its founder, Benito Quinquela Martín, intended to show in its great collection not only the work of painters from La Boca but also that of many Argentinian artists from the first half of this Century. Among them, it is worth mentioning Quinquela Martín himself, Fortunato Lacámera, Policastro, Spilimbergo, Victorica, Sívori, Gramajo Guitiérrez and Rodolfo Cascales.

On the third floor of the building, which has a superb watchtower that overlooks Vuelta de Rocha, we will find the apartment where Quinquela Martín worked and lived until the end of his life, in 1972. Upon his death, he left the whole building, including De La Ribera Theater next door, to the city's government.

"Barcazas" ("Barges"), oil painting by Quinquela Martín.

"Desde mi estudio" ("From my studio"), oil painting by Fortunato Lacámera.

Quinquela.   Filiberto.   Lacámera.

Shop of the painter Quinquela Martin in the 1st finish floor, balcony.

Terrace, sculptures exposition.

Rooms of permanent exposition.

Room of the Mascarones.

De la Ribera theatre

In the Hall of the theatre there are two important oils of Quinquela.

Opening time: Tuesday through Friday from 8 AM to 5:30 PM. Saturdays and Sundays from 8 AM to 12 and from 1 PM to 5:30 PM. Admission: free. Address: Pedro de Mendoza 1835.

La Modelo, (The Model), oil painting by Leopoldo Presas.

La utopía de mi barrio, ("The Utopia of my Neighborhood"), sculpture by Ricardo Longhini.

Mirador, acrylic painting by Rómulo Macció.

Nowadays, many painters and sculptors live and work in La Boca, which allows the quarter to preserve its tradition as a neighborhood of artists and bohemians. These are just some samples of those artists' work.

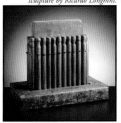

Puerto Madero and Ecological Reserve

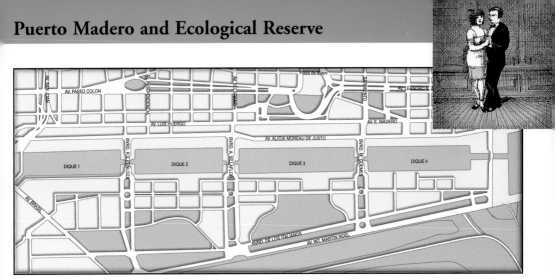

In 1880, the city's government began to build a new port, which was later given the name Puerto Madero in honor of Engineer Eduardo Madero, its designer. The project turned out to be quite similar to that of the docklands in London, with four closed and connected docks which are placed parallel to the river. In 1910, the port was already too small for the needs of a city that had increasingly gained a greater commercial activity. It was then that the so-called New Port (Puerto Nuevo) was built north of Puerto Madero. As years went by, Puerto Madero was abandoned but, in the early 1990s, a redevelopment project was carried out and the whole port became a promenade, with apartments, offices and recreation areas.

In the old redeveloped warehouses you will find a great number of restaurants (quite expensive), movie theaters, drugstores and even a University campus. We suggest that you take a walk along the docklands. The area is very attractive, both during the day and in the evening.

If you walk along Brasil street towards the river, you will pass by Ernesto de la Cárcova Art School, where you may visit the Museum of Compared Sculpture (see p. 52) and, if you turn left when you get to Costanera Avenue, you will find Las Nereidas Fountain and the Ecological Reserve (see p. 52).

Puerto Madero Dock I and II

The newly restored warehouses in Puerto Madero have preserved their original appearance for the most part. They are solid buildings made up of clay bricks in English style and they house pricey lofts that may be used as either offices or apartments. Walking along the coast in Dock I you can get a visit to the "Corbeta Uruguay" (ship).

Museum of Tracing and compared Sculpture

It is inside Ernesto de la Cárcova Art School. In the museum's rooms you will find direct reproductions of the main sculptures in the history of art. They were brought to Argentina in the beginning of this Century and, among them, we can mention some of Michelangelo's pieces (see David in the picture). When you visit the museum, you will also find perfect tracings of Egyptian relieves. Finally, we suggest that you take a walk on the cozy gardens at the back of the school, which are plenty of sculptures and mural paintings.

Malecom offices.

Cinemas.

Dock I.

Juana Manuela Gorriti

Pierina Dealessi

Elvira Rawson de Dellepiane

Julieta Lanteri

Av. Calabria

Av. Garay

Av. Brasil

Av. San Juan

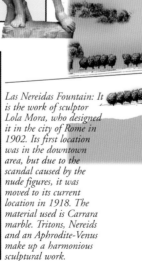

Las Nereidas Fountain: It is the work of sculptor Lola Mora, who designed it in the city of Rome in 1902. Its first location was in the downtown area, but due to the scandal caused by the nude figures, it was moved to its current location in 1918. The material used is Carrara marble. Tritons, Nereids and an Aphrodite-Venus make up a harmonious sculptural work.

El Porteño building: Luxury hotel recycled by the famous designer Philipe Starck.

Puerto Madero and Ecological Reserve

Balcarce

Carlos Calvo

Estados Unidos

Av. Independencia

Chile

Mexico

Venezuela

Av. Belgrano

Av. Ingeniero Huergo

Av. Alicia Moreau de Justo

Catholic University.

Bvd. Rosario Vera Peñaloza

Dock II.

Bvd. Azucena Villaflor

Dock III.

E. Escurra

Olga Cossettini

Petrona Eyle

Macedonia Vilotti

Pierina Dealessi

Macadizzi

Juana Manso

Maria Lynch

F. Escurra

Aime Paine

Bvd. Azucena Villaflor

Av. Calabria

Av. de los Italianos

Av. Costanera Dr. Tristán Achával Rodríguez

Del Faro Towers.

Plus Ultra dock.

De los Coipos lake.

Pergola Luis Viale.

General Office of Museums: Avenida de Los
Italianos 851. It has rooms for exhibitions
and conferences. In the 1930´s, it was a
beer pub built by Hungarian Modernist
architect Andres Kalnay.

Ecological Reserve: One of the
entrances is next to the espigón in front
of The nereidas fountain. When the
river was fulfilled with part of the
demolition of the buildings of the city,
an ecosystem was conformed. It is
similar to the one that existed before
the foundation of Buenos Aires. There is
a great variety of fauna including wild
ducks, otters and other small animals.
This is an opportunity to walk through
the "pampa" a few minutes from
the city.

Puerto Madero Dock III and IV

If we keep walking along Puerto Madero, we will reach Docks III and IV, where the best restaurants are located. Sarmiento Frigate is anchored just a few steps from there and it is open for visitors. In the area of Docks III and IV you will see modern monumental buildings.

Once you have left Puerto Madero, you may continue walking along L. N. Alem avenue, an area where you will notice many different architectural styles. This part of the city is called El Bajo or The Downward Area. In La Recova neighborhood, which runs along L. N. Alem avenue, you will find several good-quality, inexpensive restaurants.

Av. Belgrano

Defensa

Moreno

Balcarce

Adolfo Alsina

Hipólito Yrigoyen

Rivadavia

Bartolomé Mitre

Av. Paseo Colón

Av. Rosales

Av. Belgrano

Av. Ingeniero Huergo

Av. Alicia Moreau de Justo

Bvd. Azucena Villaflor

Juana Manuela Gorriti

Dique III

Bvd. Macacha Güemes

Pierina Dealessi

Olga Cossettini

Martha Lynch

Cécilia Grierson

Mangela Sáenz

Hilton Hotel

Juana Manso

Aime Paine

Trinidad Guevara

Av. de los Italianos

View of the City's buildings from the Reserve.

Puerto Madero

Bolsa de Comercio building.

Comega building.

Luna Park Stadium.

Building of "La Nación", one of the most important newspaper in Spanish.

Alas Building.

Perón

Sarmiento

Av. Corrientes

Reconquista

Mayo

Lavalle

Tucumán

Viamonte

Av. Córdoba

Av. Leandro N. Alem

Roma Square.

Bouchard

Rosales

Av. Eduardo Madero

Argentine Post office Palace: We suggest you that visit the halls.

Av. Alicia Moreau de Justo

Tourist Information Office.

Telecom building.

Dock IV

Art Museum Fortabat Foundation.

Bvd. Cecilia Grierson

Ferry to Colonia and Montevideo.

Yatching Club.

Pierina Dealessi

Victoria Ocampo

Emma de la Barra

R.Paccini de Alvear

Enriqueta Sanchez de Thompson

Opera Bay.

Yatch Club.

Juana Manso

Av. de los Italianos

Av. Costanera Intendente Carlos Noel

Ecological Reserve Costanera Sur.

Sarmiento Frigate was a training ship for the Argentine Navy. It sailed innumerable times around the world. Nowadays, it is a museum anchored in dock III.

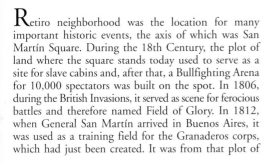

Retiro neighborhood was the location for many important historic events, the axis of which was San Martín Square. During the 18th Century, the plot of land where the square stands today used to serve as a site for slave cabins and, after that, a Bullfighting Arena for 10,000 spectators was built on the spot. In 1806, during the British Invasions, it served as scene for ferocious battles and therefore named Field of Glory. In 1812, when General San Martín arrived in Buenos Aires, it was used as a training field for the Granaderos corps, which had just been created. It was from that plot of land that the Army of the Andes departed on its mission to free Chile and Peru. The estate was finally turned into a square and named after General San Martín in 1878, for the 100th anniversary of the hero's birth.

The current landscape was designed in 1883 by French architect and landscape designer Carlos Thays. The square is on a gentle slope and on the sunny days of the year, it suddenly becomes a sunbathing spot. At the base of the slope, there stands a memorial to the soldiers that died during the war in our Malvinas (Falkland Islands) in 1982.

In the surrounding area of the square, you will find many important buildings, such as the Kavanagh (see p. 63) the Plaza Hotel, the Military Club building and San Martín Palace.

Florida street leads into the square and on its last blocks you may find many stores and shopping centers. If you walk across L.N. Alem avenue, you will reach a modern urban complex called Catalinas Norte, the most imposing group of buildings in the whole city (see p. 59). In the square's surrounding area there is a lot of cultural activity and an exciting nightlife. It is in this area that you will find the main Art Galleries in the city as well as many ethnic food restaurants and fashionable bars.

Retiro and Plaza San Martín in 3 dimensions

Military Club (Paz Palace): It was opened in 1925 and, for the time, it had a clearly academic and decadent style. It bears some resemblance with the Louvre Palace in Paris. It used to be part of a group of similar mansions that stretched along Santa Fe avenue and its surrounding area.

National Parks Service. It is one of the oldest residences that stand in the area. It was built in 1880.

National Weapons Museum: It is in the same building as the Military Club, but the entrance door to the museum is at number 745, Marcelo T. de Alvear street.
Opening time: Wednesday through Friday, 3 PM to 7 PM. Admission: $ 1.

Entrance gate to the Military Club building, wrought iron and bronze.

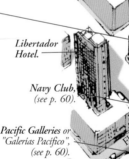

Florida street where it meets Paraguay Street.

Libertador Hotel.

Navy Club, (see p. 60).

Pacific Galleries or "Galerías Pacifico", (see p. 60).

Catalinas Convent, (see p. 60).

Claridge Hotel.

Alas Building, on Leandro N. Alem street.

Monument to General San Martín: It stands right across Santa Fe avenue and it was the first equestrian monument in the country. It was created in 1862 by French sculptor Luis José Daumas.

San Martín Palace: It is one of the seats of the Argentinian Department of State.

Kavanagh Building.
It was designed in 1935 by architects Sanchez, Lagos and De La Torre. It is 120 meters high and it once was the tallest building in South America and the first one built with reinforced concrete. Its unevenly shape was a symbol of the city for a long period. (see p. 63).

Retiro Train Station.

Tower of the British.

Plaza Hotel: It is the most traditional and luxurious hotel in the City. Designed by archtect Zucker. It offers excellent gastronomy. (see p. 63).

Sheraton Hotel.

Monument to the arrears in the war of Malvinas in the year 1982.

Basilic of the Blessed Sacrament. (see p. 63).

Catalinas Norte Urban Complex.

Florida Street. Galerías Pacífico and Borges Cultural Center in 3 dimensions

The building covers most of the area bound by Córdoba avenue, Florida street, San Martín street and Viamonte street. It was erected in the late 19th Century by architect Levacher for the purpose of housing a market called Au Bon Marché. Its designer took as a model a gallery in Milan called Vittorio Emanuelle II. After that, the building was given several purposes; it was even part of the National Museum of Fine Arts from 1896 to 1910. In the 1940s, it underwent a deep change, which altered its original appearance. From that time, there remain the excellent frescoes painted by Antonio Berni, Lino Spilimbergo, Castagnino and Colmeiro. In the 1960s, the building started to deteriorate gradually due to a lack of proper maintenance services. It was not until 1989 that restoration measures were adopted.

Nowadays, the building serves as buzzing shopping center with three stories, a big restaurant area and a movie theater.

Navy Club: It was built in 1941 and it has many richly ornamented halls. Its entrance door, on the corner of Florida street and Córdoba avenue, is entirely carved in bronze, what makes it undoubtedly magnificent.

Santa Catalina de Siena Church and Convent: The Convent was opened in 1745, it was sacked during the British Invasions and is currently empty. The Church is quite small and it has only one nave. It has been declared to be a Historical Monument.

Center Navy Building.

Av. Cordoba

San Martín

From Florida Street to Plaza de Mayo.

From Florida Street to San Martin Square.

Entrance door to the Navy Club.

Viamonte

Detail of the fountain and the mural paintings in the central area of Galerías Pacífico.

Interior of Galerías Pacífico (formerly, Au Bon Marché).

Florida Street

Florida street, between Corrientes avenue and San Martin square, has an important comercial activity and some of the most important shops in the city.

Centro Cultural Borges

In the same building of Galerias Pacifico, entering through Viamonte and San Martin streets, we can find Centro Cultural Borges. The large stairs will take to the second floor where there are a number of exhibitions rooms. There is also a library, an interactive room for children and a large auditorium.

Open from Monday to Sunday
from 10 AM to 9 PM.
Admission: $2.

View of an area of exhibition on the second floor of the Centro Cultural Borges.

Building of National Parks
Peace Palace

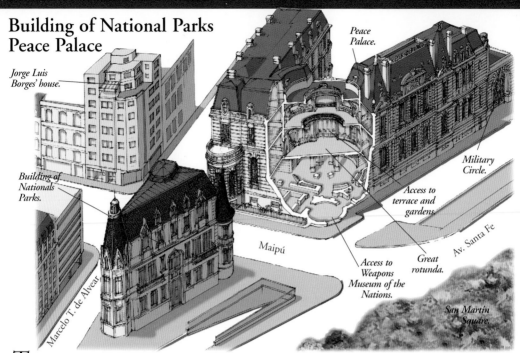

Jorge Luis Borges' house.

Peace Palace.

Building of Nationals Parks.

Military Circle.

Access to terrace and gardens.

Maipú

Av. Santa Fe

Marcelo T. de Alvear

Access to Weapons Museum of the Nations.

Great rotunda.

San Martín Square.

The Building of National Parks belonged to Villar and Haedo families and it was built by the architects Passeron and Brizuela by the end of the 19th century in Neo-gothic style. Another building that shows a luxurious and architectonic style is the Circulo Militar that was built at the beginning of the century. It belonged to the family of Jose C. Paz, the founder of La Prensa newspaper. The building was designed by the french architect Louis Sortais. In 1938, it was acquired by the Circulo Militar. It houses the National Museum of Arms where an overview of the worldwide weapons throughout the years is shown.

Anchorena Palace
Chancellery

San Martin Palace, where the ceremonies of the foreign affairs ministry are currently held, was the residence of Anchorena family until 1936. The plan was designed by the architect Alejandro Cristophersen for Mercedes Castellanos de Anchorena and her children. There is only one building with three independent residences connected to a central hall. The distinctive eclecticism of Christophersen can be seen here and there is a combination of elements of the French Academicism and Bourbon style. The Chancellery is now in a modern building crossing Esmeralda street.

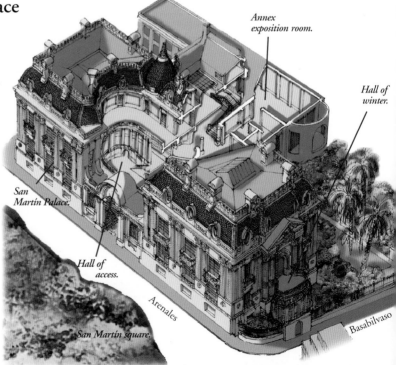

Annex exposition room.

Hall of winter.

San Martín Palace.

Hall of access.

Arenales

San Martín square.

Basabilvaso

Kavanagh Building, Basilic of the blessed Sacrament and Marriott Hotel Plaza

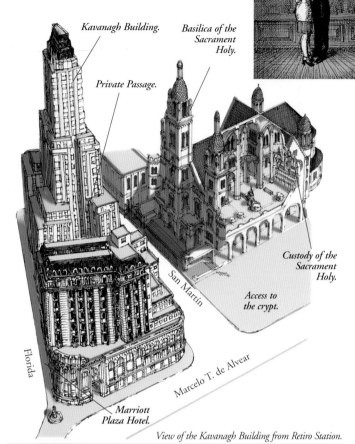

Kavanagh Building.

Basilica of the Sacrament Holy.

Private Passage.

Custody of the Sacrament Holy.

San Martín

Access to the crypt.

Florida

Marcelo T. de Alvear

Marriott Plaza Hotel.

It was opened in 1936, and for many years , it was the highest framework of reinforced concrete of the world. It was built by decision of Corina Kavanagh. This building of 120 metres, reduces in a gradual way the area of its floors, according to the rules of the codigo de edificación (building code) and ends in several terrace gardens. It was designed by the architects Sanchez, Lagos and De la Torre. It was built during 14 months and the front shows elements of the rationalist architecture. This style characterized the constructions of the 30s. The hotel Marriot Plaza is separated through a private passage, designed with the purpose of not obstructing the view from the square of the front of the Basilica del Santisimo Sacramento. It was considered a jewel of the architectonic ecclesiastical art, this church was designed by the architects Coulomb and Chauvert, then it was modified by Ernesto Vespegnani.

It was built because of the generosity of Mrs Mercedes Castellano de Anchorena whose remains are in the crypt. Its eclectic front shows reminiscense of the gothic, byzantine and romantic style and it is highlighted the sculptural group that represents the devout, julian eymard-founder of the religious group-together with two angels on their knees, made in marble. The outside enchants because of its armony and the inside is magnificent. In the crypt we can find the remains of Santiago Luis Copello, first Cardinal of Buenos Aires.

Marriot Plaza Hotel is the most stylish and exquisite building of Buenos Aires. It was designed by the architect Alfred Zucker and opened in 1909. It is a progressive work for that period. The front is highlighted and characteristics of the german baroque are shown. It has been reformed and enlarged several times throughout the years and many politicians, sportmen or sportwomen and people from the worldwide show stayed there.

View of the Kavanagh Building from Retiro Station.

Cultural and gastronomic area in 3 dimensions

The area bound by San Martín Square, Santa Fé avenue, Córdoba avenue, L.N. Alem avenue and Maipú street was the core of bustling cultural activity during the 1960s, which was encouraged by numerous cultural institutions located there. The most important ones among those institutions were Di Tella Institute and, by the end of the 1970s, the CAYC (Center for Art and Communication). However, the area is also plenty of art galleries an bars which, together with these institutions, helped create a sort of Porteño Soho that has only survived in part. Among the bars that were opened in those times, we can mention Bar Baro, on Tres Sargentos alley, and Florida Garden, at the corner of Florida and Paraguay streets. Both on San Martín street and on 25 de Mayo street, a group of post-modern and Irish bars and pubs have come up. They are all buzzing with activity in the evening, which creates a sophisticated and pleasant atmosphere. We suggest that you talk a walk in the area on Saturday morning and in the evening (See pictures).

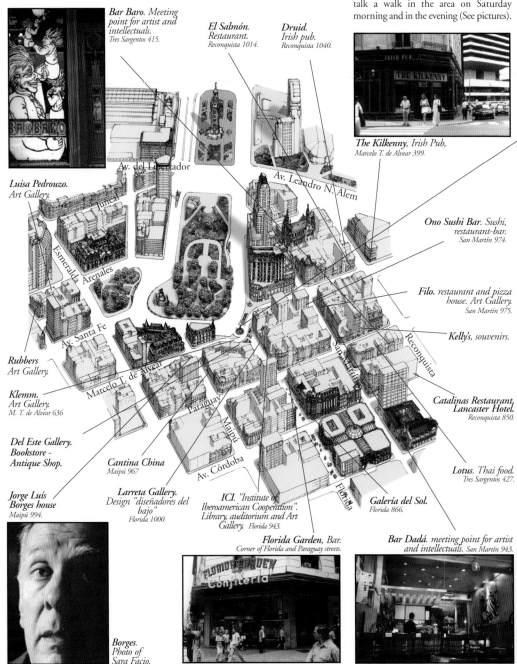

Bar Baro. Meeting point for artist and intellectuals. Tres Sargentos 415.

El Salmón. Restaurant. Reconquista 1014.

Druid. Irish pub. Reconquista 1040.

The Kilkenny, Irish Pub, Marcelo T. de Alvear 399.

Luisa Pedrouzo. Art Gallery.

Ono Sushi Bar. Sushi, restaurant-bar. San Martín 974.

Filo. restaurant and pizza house. Art Gallery. San Martín 975.

Kelly's, souvenirs.

Rubbers Art Gallery.

Klemm. Art Gallery. M. T. de Alvear 636

Catalinas Restaurant, Lancaster Hotel. Reconquista 850.

Del Este Gallery. Bookstore - Antique Shop.

Cantina China Maipú 967

Lotus. Thai food. Tres Sargentos 427.

Jorge Luís Borges house Maipú 994.

Larreta Gallery. Design "diseñadores del bajo" Florida 1000.

ICI. "Institute of Iberoamerican Cooperation". Library, auditorium and Art Gallery. Florida 943.

Galería del Sol. Florida 866.

Florida Garden, Bar. Corner of Florida and Paraguay streets.

Bar Dadá. meeting point for artist and intellectuals. San Martín 943.

Borges. Photo of Sara Facio.

Ruth Benzacar
Art Gallery. Florida 1000.

Ruth Benzacar Art Gallery houses an important collection of contemporary Argentinian paintings, among which we should mention many works by Berni.

El almuerzo. *("Lunch"), Tempera painting by Antonio Berni.*

Delfín Fitz Roy, *("Fitz Roy Dolphin") by Luis Beneditt.*

Gusanito al revés, *("Mirrored little worm"), oil painting by Jorge De La Vega.*

Alberto Greco, Egle Martin and Marta Minujín in Buenos Aires, 1964.

"La Pérdida del paraíso" ("Paradise Lost"), oil painting by Luis Felipe Noé.

Artists Rómulo Macció, Ernesto Deira, Luis Felipe Noé and Jorge De la Vega in 1963. They led a revolutionary movement in Argentinian art in the 1960s.

If you walk north on Esmeralda street from San Martín Square to Juncal street, you will find Estrogamou Palace (see p. 69). Arroyo street, with its art galleries and antiques shops starts there. This winding street finishes at Carlos Pellegrini Square, across 9 de Julio avenue. This little Parisian corner is surrounded by luxury houses, out of which the Brazilian and French Embassies and the Jockey Club stand out. These houses were built during the first decades of the 20th Century and they remind us of an opulent country, which at the time was called the "granary of the world".

The heads of the families who used to own these buildings were wealthy landowners in La Pampa. In building their houses, they forgot their taste for colonial architecture and gave the city a set of French-style mansions in an effort to imitate European aristocracy. Most of these buildings were designed by architects Rene Sergent, Lanus, Harry and Cristopherssen.

French Embassy building in front of Pellegrini Square at the beginning of Alvear avenue.

Access through Duhau Palace. One of the most luxurious of the city.

Armani. One of the many places that make Alvear avenue exclusive.

Av. Callao

Alvear Hotel.

Av. Alvear

Ayacucho

Schiaffino

Alvear Square.

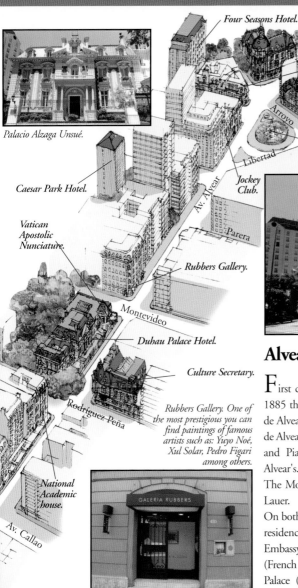

Four Seasons Hotel.

French Embassy.

Alzaga Unzue Palace.

Brazilian Embassy.

Palacio Alzaga Unsué.

Arroyo

Libertad

Carlos Pellegrini Square.

Caesar Park Hotel.

Av. Alvear

Jockey Club.

Vatican Apostolic Nunciature.

Parera

Rubbers Gallery.

Montevideo

Duhau Palace Hotel.

Culture Secretary.

Rubbers Gallery. One of the most prestigious you can find paintings of famous artists such as: Yuyo Noé, Xul Solar, Pedro Figari among others.

Rodríguez Peña

National Academic house.

Av. Callao

GALERIA RUBBERS

Palacio Atucha.

Alvear Avenue in 3 dimensions

First called Bella Vista, Alvear Avenue was designed in 1885 through Buenos Aires' first Mayor, Don Torcuato de Alvear's initiative, in honour to his father, Carlos Maria de Alvear. It starts in front of Carlos Pellegrini's Monument and Piazza and ends in front of Mayor Torcuato de Alvear's.

The Monument inaugurated in 1900 was made by Juan Lauer.

On both sides of Alvear avenue stand beautiful homes and residences like Pereda Family Palace (at present the Embassy of Brazil), Ortiz Basualdo Family Residence (French Embassy) and Concepcion Unzue de Casares Palace (at present the Jockey Club premises) and the Residences of Atucha and Alzaga Unzue Families which are now integrated to the Four Seasons Hotel.

The above mentioned buildings lead to Carlos Pellegrini Piazza where Alvear Avenue finds its urban axis and limits all excelling in their French architecture bringing about an unprecedented Parisian image.

At the intersection of Alvear Avenue and Ayacucho we find Alvear Palace Hotel, one of of our finest expressions in hotel services. Built in 1928 by Engineer Escudero y Ortuzar and Architects Valentin Brodski and Estanislao Pirovano, its 11 floors and 280 rooms, decorated in different styles, show great comfort and high quality expressions of finesse and good taste.

Victorian Palace in the corner of Alvear avenue and Rodríguez Peña street.

Retiro and Alvear Avenue in 3 dimensions

Duhau Residence and Apostolic Nunciature: They make up a well-matching group of three mansions on Alvear avenue. The Apostolic Nunciature was built by architect Le Monnier and it served as residence for popes Pius XII and John Paul II during their visits to Buenos Aires.

Del Infinito Art Gallery.

Carlos Pellegrini Square: Undoubtedly, it is the most French-styled square you will find in Buenos Aires. It is surrounded by a large group of examples of rationalist architecture built during the 1930s. The central area of the square is crowned by a monument to Dr Carlos Pellegrini, former Argentinian President. The Jockey Club, a prestigious institution that follows the style of the most exclusive English clubs, lies in front of the square. It has a huge and valuable library.

Detail of the top floor in Lenguas Vivas School. It stands on Carlos Pellegrini avenue, across from Hyatt Hotel.

The place were the Embassy of Israel was located, in the corner of Arroyo and Suipacha streets. After the tragic attack in 1992; a commemorative square was built where you can see the characteristics of the old embassy.

Painting by Octavio Pinto, one of the most important landscape painters in Argentina. Some of his pieces may be seen at Mercedes Pinto art gallery.

Palatina: traditional gallery in Arroyo street. It has important paintings from Petorutti, Torres Garcia, Gurvich and Alonso.

Vasari Art Gallery. Esmeralda 1357.

Patio Bullrich: *It is a classy shopping center. Inside it, you may find some traces of the old, renovated building, which used to serve as location for livestock auctions. It has an entrance door on Posadas street and another one on Libertador avenue. In the building, there is a movie theater and some sophisticated restaurants, such as Cipriani, on Posadas street.*

Caesar Park Hotel.

Restaurants on Posadas street and 9 de Julio avenue: *From Four Seasons Hotel, under the highway, the main Argentinian gourmets have opened their restaurants to offer different kinds of food to the public. The services are quite expensive. Across the street from the restaurant area, you will find Zurbarán Gallery, one of the main art galleries in the city specialized in Argentinian art.*

Sofitel Hotel. *Bar and restaurant. Arroyo 845.*

Arroyo Street: *Art gallery and antiquary area among others, Palatina gallery, Zabaleta Lab, Mercedes Pinto, Agustina del Campo, Arroyo, Praxis and Principium; on Fridays you can enjoy Gallery Nights visited by a lot of people.*

Mercedes Pinto. *Contemporary Art. Arroyo and Suipacha streets.*

Arroyo. *Art Gallery. Arroyo 830*

Estrugamou Palace, *It was built in 1922 by architects Sauze and Mouguier. It is a apartment building with suites covering 500 to 600 square meters. The building material was exported from France and, if you peer into the entrance hall, you will find a bronze reproduction of the Victory of Samothrace, a treasure of the Louvre in Paris.*

Museum of Spanish-American Art Isaac Fernandez Blanco

The former Noel Palace is currently the seat for our Museum of Spanish-American Art. It was built in the 1920s by architect Martin Nöel, founder of the neocolonial architectural style. The main building, surrounded by gardens, has balconies with closings and fences in wrought iron. It houses the museum's pieces, among which we can mention a colonial silverware collection that is thought to be the most important one in the continent. The library is an interesting spot with its baroque boiserie, where valuable religious objects are on exhibition. The gardens make the perfect place to relax among the high-rise apartment buildings in the area. The Museum is located at Suipacha 1422 between Avenida del Libertador and Arroyo street.

Opening time:
Tuesday through Sunday, 2 PM to 7 PM.
Admission: $ 2.

Folkloric engraving dating from the early 19th Cent.

Recoleta

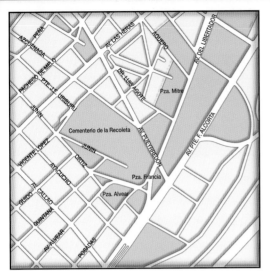

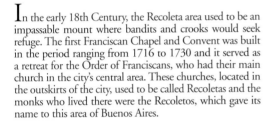

In the early 18th Century, the Recoleta area used to be an impassable mount where bandits and crooks would seek refuge. The first Franciscan Chapel and Convent was built in the period ranging from 1716 to 1730 and it served as a retreat for the Order of Franciscans, who had their main church in the city's central area. These churches, located in the outskirts of the city, used to be called Recoletas and the monks who lived there were the Recoletos, which gave its name to this area of Buenos Aires.

People started to settle down in this area in 1870, when the cholera and yellow fever plagues brought wealthy families from the southern areas of the city to the north region.

The neighborhood acquired a sumptuous appearance in 1885, when Alvear avenue was built and mansions, squares and parks started to come up along it.

Behind the Church of Recoleta, there used to be an area covered with slaughterhouses and stockyards, where carts coming from the northern zones of the country would stop. It served as a meeting point for country laborers and outcasts and it was in this environment, plenty of cafeterias, general stores and tenement houses that tango music is thought to have been born. This is the place where the mythical Armenonville was located, on the corner of Libertador avenue and Tagle street. This and the Palais de Glace were the main tango ballrooms in the country.

Out tour, which comes from Alvear avenue in Retiro, will take us left to San Martín de Tours Park, a lovely place full of enormous magnolia trees. If we walk across the park to our right, we will find the cemetery, the Church of Pilar and the Recoleta Cultural Center. After that, if we walk across Francia Square, we will reach the National Museum of Fine Arts and further along a tree-covered Libertador avenue, we will find the National Library and the Museum of Decorative and Eastern Arts.

Recoleta in 3 dimensions

Basilica of our lady of Pilar.

Construction began in 1716 and the church was consecrated in 1732. Its harmonious facade with pilasters and cornices is crowned by a discreet tympanum and a lateral tower that reaches 30 meters high. Inside the church you will find just one nave surrounded by niches where the smaller altars are placed. The main altarpiece was brought from northern Peru and it has a wrought-silver frontal made by Native Americans from Jujuy. The church also has a lot of interesting religious icons, such as the Christ of Humility and Patience, a Crucified Christ by sculptor Martinez Montañés, and one of the few images of San Francisco de Paola which have remained in the city.

Building of the Car Argentine Club, in racionalist style.

Intendente Alvear Square:

It is located across the Church of Pilar. If we walk across this square, we will run into Ortiz pedestrian walk, along which there are several restaurants. Going to La Biela for some coffee in the evening is a must. The hundred-year-old rubber plant in the square is the biggest one in the city. Its crown is over 70 meters wide and the tree itself is over 20 meters high. The tree's scientific name is Ficus macrophylla and it was brought from Australia. The square has recently been renovated and, during the weekend, it serves as a huge outdoors theater plenty of mimes, tango dancers and street performers.

La Biela Café, on the corner of Quintana and Ortiz streets.

Cementery of the Recoleta.

Agüero

Agüer

Laprida

Galileo

Galileo

Gelly Obes

Luis Agote

Guido

Av. Las Heras

Av. Pueyrredón

Azcuénaga

Engineering University.

Village Recoleta Cinemas and restaurants. Cúspide bookshop.

Uriburu

Vte. López

Junín

Loi Suite Hotel, restaurant and bar. Vicente López 1955. Tel.: 5777-8950

Restaurants on Ortiz pedestrian walk, between Quintana and Guido street.

Guido

Ayacucho

Quintana

It is on the left side of the Church and it originally was the Convent's garden and orchard. In 1822, engineer Felipe Bertres designed the plans for a new cemetery in the northern area of the city. In 1828, Governor Manuel Dorrego made the cemetery bigger till it reached its current size. Along the cemetery's streets, you will find mausoleums with sculptures by famous local and international artists. Many well-known people are buried here, such as Eva Duarte de Perón, Domingo Faustino Sarmiento, Juan Manuel de Rosas, Facundo Quiroga and Bartolomé Mitre among others.

Recoleta

National Museum of
Decorative and
Eastern Arts
(see pages 80 and 81).

Peluca Lucena

National Library
(see pages 78 and 79).

Tagle

Austria

Agüero

Bustamante

Av. del Libertador

Av. Figueroa Alcorta

Statue of General Mitre.
The terrace around it, works
as a perfect watchtower.

Floralis generica.
Enourmous titanium
flower with opening
and closing automatic
system. (See piture in
page 70).

Monument given
by the French
government to the
Argentinian one,
located in front of
the Museum of
Fine Arts.

Law School,
opened in 1936.
Its neoclasical
and germanic
style was liked by
the military
government of
the moment.

National Museum
of Fine Arts
(pages 76 and 77).

Monument to Brigadier Gral. Carlos M. de Alvear

It was created by French sculptor Emile Antoine Bourdelle and it is one of the most interesting equestrian statues in the city. It was unveiled in 1925. There are many pieces by the same artist scattered around the park across the street from this monument.

Av. del Libertador

Av. Figueroa Alcorta

Posadas

El centauro herido,
(The Wounded
Centaur) by
Antoine
Bourdelle.

Palais de Glace.
Art center.

Alvear Hotel,
one of the largest
and traditional
of the city. It
has excellent
restaurants.

Recoleta
Cultural Center
(see pages 74 and 75).

San Martin de Tours
Square, it has an
area covered by
magnolia trees.

Torso, by
colombian sculptor,
Fernando Botero.

Recoleta Cultural Center in 3 dimensions

Este This building was originally meant to be a Franciscan Convent and it was designed in the middle-18th Century period by Brother Blanqui.

In 1858, it was enlarged and renovated by Juan Buschiazzo and, after that, it became a house for beggars and older people. The people who lived in this house were evicted in 1979 and the building became a Cultural center. The second renovation project was undertaken by architects Clorindo Testa, Luis Benedit and Jaques Bedel. If you walk down the entrance hall to your right, you will get to the old cloisters, which surround three patios in a row. Doing this will allow you to visit part of the original building. This area is currently devoted to exhibitions that are regularly renewed. At the end of the long corridor you will find a room where experimental theater plays are usually performed.

If you walk through the patio in front of the entrance hall, you will find three special exhibition halls. One of them is called Cronopios and the other two adjoining rooms have recently been renovated, provided with equipment and conditioned. These are the halls where exhibitions by professional artists from Argentina and from abroad are usually held. There is also an auditorium right where the old chapel used to be, which was adapted to the needs of modern show halls. On the first floor, there is an interactive science museum for children. Visiting the cultural center will be an interesting experience, no matter what day of the week you do it. You will always find it buzzing with activity and shows, as well as the square in front of the entrance hall.

Behind the cultural center, you will see the Hard Rock Café, which has its entrance door on Pueyrredón avenue. If you walk along the path that is covered with trees to the right of the cultural center, you will get to a restaurant promenade where a wide range of food services is offered. Finally, if you go down on the comfortable escalator, you will enter "Buenos Aires Design", a shopping center exclusively devoted to furniture, household appliances and design objects.

View of the exhibition halls with the original vaulted ceiling.

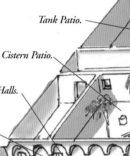

Tank Patio.

Cistern Patio.

Exhibition Halls.

Entrance stairway to the first floor.

Fountain Patio.

Church of Pilar.

View of the O.A.S. Building.

Orange Trees Patio.

View of the Recoleta Cultural Center facade and entrance door.

Linden Trees Patio.

Entrance door to Cronopios hall and Interactive Science Museum.

Recoleta

View of the old chapel (today, an auditorium).

Many people visit the exhibitions during the weekend.

Window to the Fountain Patio.

Hard Rock Cafe building.

Uvo, *oil painting on canvass by Enzo Cuchi.*

View of the restaurant area.

Las alas del deseo, *(The Wings of Desire), acrylic on canvass by Carlos Gorriarena.*

Entrance to Buenos Aires Design.

Tótem, *Sculpture by Hernan Dompe.*

National Museum of Fine Arts in 3 dimensions

Orquesta típica *(Typical Orchestra) by Antonio Berni.Antonio Berni.*

In 1930, architect Bustillo adapted the building that used to house the water pumps of the city so that it would become the current seat for the National Museum of Fine Arts.

This museum covers an area of over 10,000 square meters and it has over 10,000 works of art in its collection. It houses a permanent exhibition in which you may appreciate the most important and exhaustive collection of Argentinian sculpture and painting from the 19th and 20th Centuries. On the ground floor, you will find European paintings from every period, sculptures, paintings and tapestries from the pre-Renaissance period, the Renaissance period and the 17th, 18th and 19th Centuries. This also includes a wide range of impressionist and post-impressionist pieces.

The most important works are a series of war scenes by Goya, La Ninfa sorprendida (The Surprised Nymph) by Manet, La Crucifixión (The Crucifixion) by Lucas Cranach, El Retrato (The Portrait) attributed to Rembrandt, and other paintings by El Greco, Titian, Gauguin, an excellent Picasso, some works by Modigliani, Tapies, Saura, Sironi, etc.

La Urpila *(The Small Dove) by Ramón Gomez Cornet, 1946.*

Second Floor: Direction, Administrative Offices and temporary exhibitions.

First Floor: Argentinian Art, 19th and 20th Centuries.

Figura *(Figure) by Lino Enea Spilimbergo, 1938.*

Crucifijo procesional *(Processional Crucifix) anonymous in gold, bronze and crystal, 18th Century.*

Retrato de la hermana *(Portrait of Sister) by Rembrandt van Rijn.*

Secretario *(Secretary) by Titian Vecelli.*

Desembarco del ejército en Curuzú *(Landing of the Curuzú Troops) by Cándido López.*

Recoleta

Untitled, *by Antonio Seguí, 1987.*

*La ninfa sorprendida
(The Surprised Nymph)
by Edouard Manet.*

En el camino dos
*(On the road two)
by Juan Carlos
Distéfano, 1980.*

Temporary Exhibitions Wing.

La mujer del mar
*(The Lady of the Sea)
by Paul Gauguin.*

Amarillo y Rosa
*(yellow and pink).
Edgar Degas.*

**Down floor: European
art, Pre-renaissance,
Centuries XVI, XVII, XVIII, XIX, XX.**

La crucifixión de
Cristo *(The
Crucifixion of
Christ) by Lucas
Cranach.*

El beso
*(The Kiss)
by Auguste Rodin.*

Busto de mujer
*(Female Bust)
by Amadeo
Modigliani.*

National Library

Across the street from the library, you will find a wide extension of parks.

It is located on the plot of land of the former Presidential Residence, where its last inhabitant, Eva Perón, passed away.

Construction of the library started in the 1950s and, after many delays and difficulties, it was finally opened in 1992. The building was designed by architects Clorindo Testa, Bullrich and Cazaniga. It is situated in the center of a huge garden and it has entrance doors on Austria street and Agüero street. The building's basis is an enormous esplanade from which you can enjoy a bird's eye view of Libertador avenue and the adjoining parks.

The book storage area is located under this esplanade. It has three underground levels and it may store up to 5 million copies. An elevator will take you to the exhibition hall and the reading room, an immense suite two stories high with magnificent views of the city.

On the first underground level, you will find a valuable collection of national and local newspapers and magazines. The reading room is spacious and informal.

The old library used to be located on México street, in San Telmo quarter and it was founded in 1810. Jorge Luis Borges was director of the National Library between the 1950s and the 1970s. The new library organizes a wide variety of events, both in its exhibition hall and in the auditorium it houses.

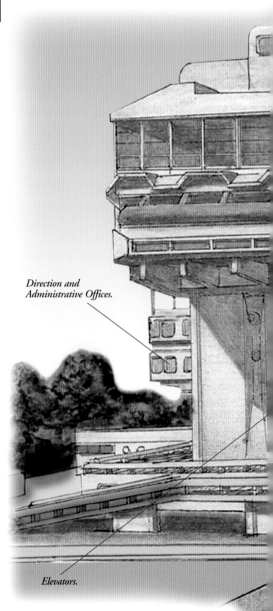

Direction and Administrative Offices.

Elevators.

Library building as seen from Libertador avenue.

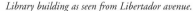

Map Collection.

Reading Room.

Exhibition Hall.

Jorge Luis Borges Auditorium.

Esplanade.

Entrance doors.

Newspaper and Magazin Collection.

Storages.

National Museum of Art Deco in 3 dimensions

Façade of the museum.

Rococo-inspired entrance door.

Vista de Roma *(View of Rome), oil painting by Jean B. Corot.*

Pereyra Lucena

Av. del Libertador

Wrought iron and bronze entrance gate in Louis XVI style.

National Museum of Decorative and Eastern Arts in 3 Dimensions Palace Errázuriz houses the National Museum of Decorative and Eastern Arts. The project was developed by prestigious French architect Rene Sergent, who never visited Buenos Aires and yet designed most of the best mansions in the city, such as those of the Alvear family and Ernesto Bosch's. The building is designed in a French style typical of the late 18th Century period and it reminds us of the chateaux that make up the Place de la Concorde in Paris.

You may enter the museum through a wrought iron and bronze entrance gate in Louis XVI style. Once inside of the building, you will find a series of halls that have been decorated in different styles from different periods. Thus, in the first place you will find the entrance patio in Louis XVI style, then you will enter the huge reception hall in Renaissance style, a suite that has unique dimensions (20 meters long, 18 meters wide and over 10 meters high). This hall has been decorated by Nelson. Pay special attention to the magnificent fireplace and the immense windows on its sides.

Other interesting rooms in the museum are the greenhouse and the Regencia hall.

The permanent exhibition displays valuable pieces from the museum's collection, including 18th Century objects, sculptures and paintings. The museum also organizes special events and exhibitions.

La condesa de las cuevas de Vera *(The countess of the Caves of Saw), oil of Anglada Camarassa.*

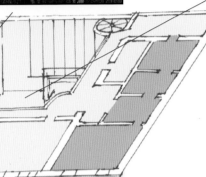

Entrance hall decorated by Nelson. View of the magnificent fireplace carved in stone.

Louis XVI bureau and Chinese vases in Kang Hi style.

Desvanecimiento de la Virgen, *(Fai carving, 15th Century).*

Virgen con el niño y San Juan Bautista, *(Virgin and Child with St John Baptist), Renaissance oil painting on woo. Jacopo dell'Sellaio.*

Bustamante

Museum of Eastern Arts

The Museum of Eastern Arts is located on the first floor of the building and it has many valuable collections of pottery, lacquerwork, engravings and furniture.

In the entrance to the museum you will find a cozy restaurant-bar with an excellent atmosphere. On the main house's basement, you will find a bookshop and souvenir store.

Virgen María, *talla policromada siglo XIV. Policromated carving of Virgin Maria. 19th Century.*

Address: *Avenida del Libertador 1962, between Pereyra Lucena and Bustamante streets. From Monday to Sunday from3 PM to 7 PM.* **Admission: $2.**

81

Palermo

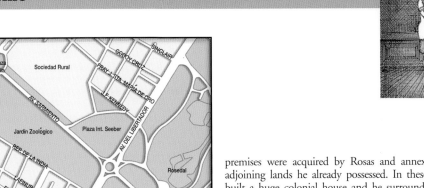

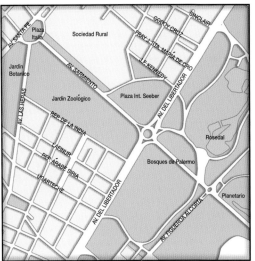

premises were acquired by Rosas and annexed to the adjoining lands he already possessed. In these fields he built a huge colonial house and he surrounded it with cages that housed exotic animals, which he designed to impress and entertain his visitors. This way, he gave birth to a style that would be imitated by many South American dictators and caudillos.

In 1872, under the initiative of President Sarmiento, Tres de Febrero Park was founded. The complex was made up of a series of gardens: a zoo, a botanical garden, a rose garden and the so-called Palermo Woods, decorated with artificial lakes. Undoubtedly, this is the greatest green area in the city and it will allow us to take a long walk in close contact with nature. There is a wide variety of trees and plants from different parts of the country, some hidden corners and gazebos next to the lakes are undoubtedly charming. We suggest you take this tour on a special sunny day and go to the Planetarium and the Sívori Museum.

In the early 17th Century, the northern area of the city was covered by lowlands and swamps that were easily flooded. A Sicilian man called Juan Palermo bought this land for agricultural purposes and he gave it the name of "Palermo Fields". It was only later, around 1820, that these

Palermo in 3 dimensions

Sivori Museum

It is an important museum of Argentinian painting, sculpture, engraving and illustration from the 19th and 20th Centuries. Its huge collection is only partly exhibited in this newly opened branch. Temporary exhibitions are also held in this museum. It is located in Av. de la Infanta 555.

> Opening time:
> Tuesday through Friday,
> 12 to 6 PM. Admission: $1.

El Infernillo (The Spirit Lamp), oil painting by Marcia Schvartz.

José León Pagano, bronze, 1936.

Los Rosedales (The Rose Gardens). You may get to the rose gardens either walking along an avenue surrounded by flowerbeds or crossing a bridge upon the lake. There are many interesting spots in the rose gardens, such as the Poet's Corner, the Andalucian Patio, the roses area and a magnificent gazebo that looks upon the lake. These gardens are plenty of visitors during the weekend.

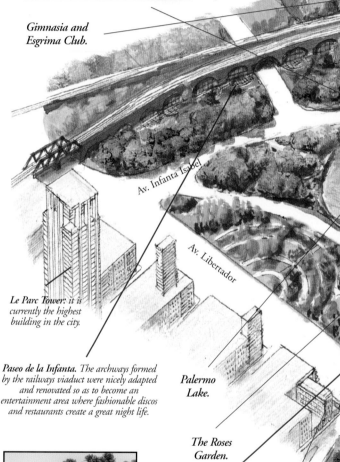

Gimnasia and Esgrima Club.

Av. Infanta Isabel

Av. Libertador

Le Parc Tower: it is currently the highest building in the city.

Paseo de la Infanta. The archways formed by the railways viaduct were nicely adapted and renovated so as to become an entertainment area where fashionable discos and restaurants create a great night life.

Palermo Lake.

The Roses Garden.

The Poet's Garden.

Residence of the U.S. Embassy.

Int. Seeber Square.

Among the indigenous species of the Patagonic area we find the Araucaria tree.

Palermo

Galileo Galilei Planetarium

This building has a theater that sits 360 people, it is properly equipped and, on its vaulted ceiling, images of the cosmos are projected. It also serves as location for scientific events and shows. A valuable metallic meteorite is exhibited on the entrance esplanade. It fell on the province of Chaco in 1965. The Planetarium is located on the corner of Sarmiento and Figueroa Alcorta avenues.

Opening time:
Monday through Sunday, from 10 AM to 6 PM.
Guided Tours:
Saturdays and Sundays at 3 PM,
4:30 PM and 6 PM.
Admission:
$ 5 for adults and $ 3 for children.

Tennis Club.

Av. Figueroa Alcorta

Av. Libertador

Av. Sarmiento

Monument to Sarmiento
Designed by famous French sculptor Auguste Rodin, the monument has been erected right where the house of Rosas used to stand, which is curious since he was President Sarmiento's bitterest enemy.

Zoo Garden
(see p. 86).

Monument to the Spaniards
It is a complex sculptural work finally carved in marble. It is 25 meters high and it was erected by the city as a way to honor Spanish residents.

Plaza Italia (Italy Square), Botanical Garden, Zoo and Rural Exhibition Center

Travelling by subway from the downtown area on line D, we stop at the Plaza Italia Metro Station. On the main route of this walk, the equestrian statue of Garibaldi stands out. On the right, we find the access to the Botanical Garden (see this page). Facing it, across Las Heras Avenue, is the main entrance to the Zoo (see p. 83) and on the opposite side of Sarmiento Avenue, there is a big exhibition center. Among the most important exhibitions thas take place there are the Buenos Aires Book Fair, ARTEBA, an important fair of art galleries, and the rural exhibition, an extremely interesting agricultural and livestock exhibition. Sarmiento Avenue ends right in the middle of Plaza Italia and if we walk 656 yards, we will bump into the Spaniards Monument and beyond it, the Palermo Forest.

Excursion Office, British style brick architecture. It is located in the stroll main access.

The Botanical Garden

Designed by the famous landscape designer Carlos Thays, it was inaugurated in 1902. The main entrance is at the corner of Santa Fe and Las Heras. From there on, you may walk through the main landscape route to the large greenhouse, a building that received an award in the International Exhibition of Paris. Beside it, lies a brick building, now the Excursion Office (dirección de paseos). Several sculptures decorate this area and among them, stands out Ondina del Plata by the sculptur Lucio Correa Morales. Open Tuesday to Sundays at 10 a.m.

Greenhouse of iron and crystal.

Av. Las Heras

Gutierrez

Rep. Arabe Siria

Rep. de la India

Cabello

Lafinur

Av. Cervino

J. F. Segui

Av. Libertador

Monument to the Spaniards.

Monument to Domingo F. Sarmiento.

Palermo

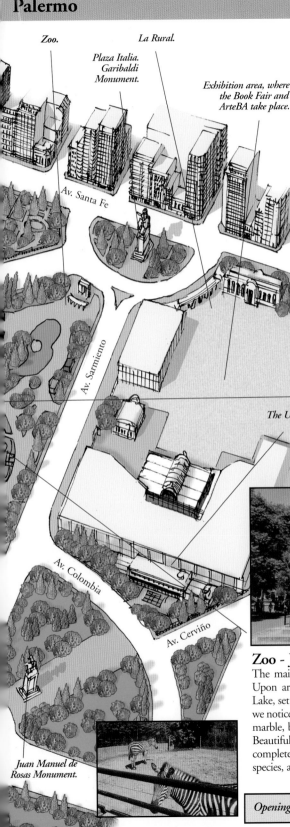

Zoo.

Plaza Italia.
Garibaldi
Monument.

La Rural.

Exhibition area, where
the Book Fair and
ArteBA take place.

Av. Santa Fe

Av. Sarmiento

Av. Colombia

Av. Cerviño

Juan Manuel de
Rosas Monument.

The United States
Embassy.

Front of Evita
Museum on
Lafinur street.

Evita Museum

This neo colonial palace houses a museum that in an entertaining and didactic way tells the life and work of Eva Perón, one of the most important and influential women of the 20th century. There are dress collections, works of art, and a complete documentation archive. The libarary and archive files of the Eva Perón Institute that operates there, are also available for consultation. In the museum's patio there is a cozy bar and restaurant.

Opening time: Tuesdays to Fridays from 2 PM to 7:30 PM.
Lafinur 2988

Zoo - Jardín Zoológico

The main entrance is at the Las Heras an Sarmiento Arcade. Upon arrival we encounter a panoramic view of the Darwin Lake, set in a romantic landscape of the 19th century. The ruins we notice on the isle of this lake, are made of authentic Byzantine marble, brought from Trieste in 1910. The Elephant Palace is a Beautiful Indian fantasy. japanese pagodas and Roman shrines complete a didactic imaginary stroll. There is a wide variety of species, as well as an aquarium and Snake Exhibit.

Opening time: Tuesday to Sunday from 10 AM to 6 PM.

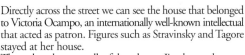

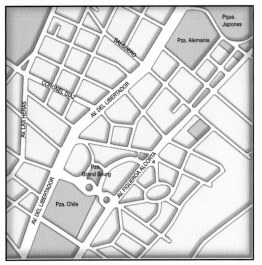

Si The area layout was designed by Carlos Thays and it was built in 1912.

If we move forward through Libertador Avenue, leaving behind the Decorative Art Museum; once we've crossed the avenue, we will arrive at an ancient grove area, among which we find grand residences and aristocratic palaces, many of them Embassies, such as the Embassy of Spain, Belgium, and Portugal.

Turning on Mariscal Castilla street, and just one block further, we will see the Grand Bourg House: a reproduction of the place where General San Martín lived his last years (see p. 90).

Directly across the street we can see the house that belonged to Victoria Ocampo, an internationally well-known intellectual that acted as patron. Figures such as Stravinsky and Tagore stayed at her house.

Through a pleasant walk of densely tree-lined curved streets, we arrive at Figueroa Alcorta Avenue at the intersection of San Martín de Tours street, where the Latin American Art Museum is located. (MALBA) (see page 92).

One block further, crossing Salguero Avenue, there is a giant Shopping Center (Paseo Alcorta), where we will find an inexpensive food terrace and amusement areas.

Walking on through Figueroa Alcorta towards the north, we find the entrance to the Japanese Garden, a peaceful oriental oasis. It is worth mentioning there is a big lake full of fishes and ducks, set among footbridges and a Japanese pavilion. Together it all forms a wonderfullandscape. There is a tea-house and an active Japanese Cultural Center.

Facing the Japanese Park, on the other side of Casares Avenue, is the Plaza Alemania (German Park). In the center of the park, there's a monument of severe lines, a creation of the sculptor Gabredón, made in 1914. It was all donated to the Argentine Republic by the German community.

Towards the south, at number 2373, we will find the José Hernández Argentine Crafts Museum (see page 91).

Palermo Chico in 3 dimensions

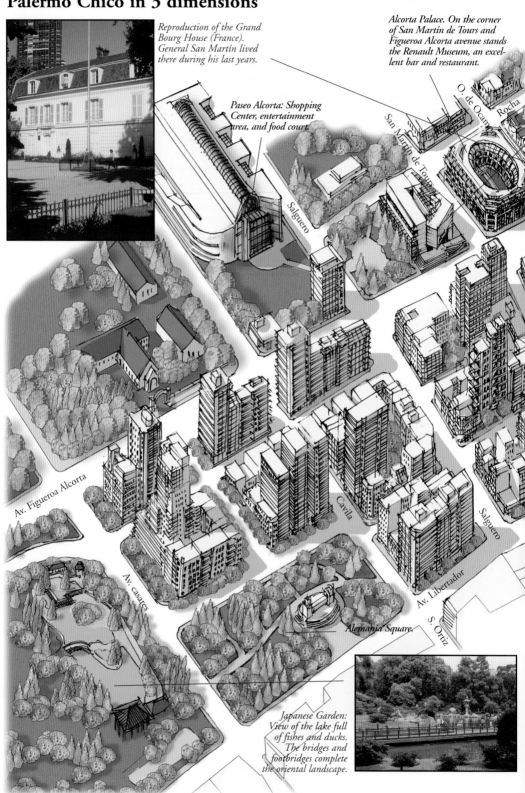

Reproduction of the Grand Bourg House (France). General San Martín lived there during his last years.

Paseo Alcorta: Shopping Center, entertainment area, and food court.

Alcorta Palace. On the corner of San Martín de Tours and Figueroa Alcorta avenue stands the Renault Museum, an excellent bar and restaurant.

O. de Ocam

Rocha

San Martín de Tours

Salguero

Av. Figueroa Alcorta

Av. casates

Cavila

Salguero

Av. Libertador

S. Ortíz

Alemania Square.

Japanese Garden: View of the lake full of fishes and ducks. The bridges and footbridges complete the oriental landscape.

Latin American Art Museum
(MALBA), *(see p. 92).*

*Victoria
Ocampo*

General San
Martín
Monument.

Av. Figueroa Alcorta

Costa

M. Castilla

Coronel Diaz

Q. de Ocampo

Av. Libertador

San Martín de Tours Church.

MAMAN Art Gallery.
*Contemporary art.
Av. del Libertador 2475.*

*Victoria Ocampo's House. Promotor of the arts.
Founder of Sur magazine. She built one of the
first recionalist houses, nowadays it is
administrated by National Fund of Arts. There
are exhibitions, conferences and concerts.*

*Under a dense green cloak,
some luxurious houses can be
seen. This area was designed
by the landscape architect,
Carlos Thays. This urban
development was built in
1912, many of the palaces are
now embassies. It's the most
exclusive area of the city.*

**"Jose Hernández"
Argentine Craft Museum**
*It houses a wide collection of Creole
Silverware from the 19th century
and there is also an exhibition of
crafts from the provinces. The
library is focused on folklore and
can be consulted.*

Opening time: *Tuesday to Friday
from 2 PM to 7 PM. Saturday
and Sunday from 3 PM to 7 PM.
Avda. del Libertador 2376.*

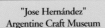

MALBA Museum in 3 dimensions

Latin American Art Museum.
Constantini Collection.

> *Opemimg time:*
> *every day except tuesdays.*
> *Wednesday: free.*
> *Admission: $4.*
> *Av. Figueroa Alcorta 3415.*

In a modern building lies the recently inaugurated Latin American Art Museum of Buenos Aires. It houses the Constantini Collection, one of the few private cultural enterprises; absolutely remarkable. Works by the main Latin American painters and sculptors can be seen in its permanent exhibition room. From Botero to Frida Kahlo, and also the Argentines Antonio Berni and Xul Solar, who are very well represented in this collection. The museum also offers a great cultural activity through films, videos, documentaries and conferences. For this purpose, it houses a spacious auditorium and a fully-equipped library.

In the ground floor hall, there's a cozy bar with a nice view and good food. Opposite to it, there is a complete bookstore that also sells works of art made by local artists at affordable prices.

Façade on Figueroa Alcorta Avenue.

Escalators take visitors to the permanent exhibition rooms on the first and second floor.

Temporary Exhibition Hall.

Permanent Collection Room.

Bar & Restaurant.

Hall & Information Point.

View of the Exhibition Rooms on the second floor.

malba | colección costantini

Av. Figueroa Alcorta

Access.

Bookstore.

Palermo Chico

Manifestación, *(Demostration), Antonio Berni, Oil, 1934.*

Composición simetrica universal, *(Universal Symmetric Composition), J. Torres García, Oil, 1931.*

Water Patio.

Sculptures Terrace.

Los premios, *(The Awards), Ernesto Deira, Oil and enamel, 1963.*

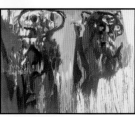

Composición, *(Composition), Carmelo Arden Quin, óleo and wood, 1945.*

San Martín de Tours

Library.

Untitled, *León Ferrari, Steel wire, 1984.*

La canción del pueblo, *(The People's Song), Emilio Pettoruti, Oil, 1927.*

Los cuatro, *(The Four), Xul Solar, water colour, 1921.*

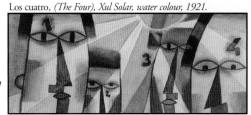

View of the spacious Access Hall.

Foyer, auditorium and temporary exhibitions.

Autorretrato con mono y loro, *(Self-portrait with Monkey and Parrot), Frida Kahlo, Oil, 1942.*

Ábaporu, *Tarsila do amaral, Oil, 1928.*

Palermo Viejo / Las Cañitas

Going to the north, through Córdoda or Las Heras avenue to Plaza Italia we arrive to Palermo Viejo. In the 3500 block of Córdoba you can turn right and you will arrive to a neighborhood of one or two story houses, simple and recycled with good taste. Nowadays, it is a middle and high class neigborhood with a sophisticated commercial circuit specialized in gastronomy, fasion and design. This zone inspired great writers, such as Julio Cortázar that uses this zone as part of his novel Rayuela and the square of the place takes his name. On the other hand, Jorge Luis Borges imagined here the mythic foundation of Buenos Aires.

Armenia street reveals the presence of this community in part of the area with its Orthodox Church that is surrounded by a number of institutions administrated by them.

Palermo Viejo has its center in Plaza Julio Cortázar surrounded by discos, bars, restaurants, art galleries, articles of design, bookstores and boutiques. The place has an intensive life that starts in the afternoon till late at night. There are ethnic restaurants with a great variety of prices.

The neighborhood goes on to Godoy Cruz street where we Palermo Hollywood that has the same characteristics of Palermo Viejo.

Santa Rosa Passage on the corner of Jorge Luis Borges street. Another characteristic of the neighborhood are the narrow streets that go between Gurruchaga and Thames streets. They have gastronomy and design houses and shops

Miles/Prometeo Music and books.

Soler street to the north. Many of Palermo Viejo´s streets still have trees that make the space very fresh in summer.

Traditional bar Malasartes in Honduras 4999.

San Francisco Javier Church.

Bar and art gallery El Taller. Traditional meeting place.

Mythic foundation of Buenos Aires.

Map labels: Cat, Gorriti, Honduras, El Salvador, Costa Rica, Nicaragua, Av. Scalabrini Ortiz, Soler, Plaza Palermo Viejo, Guatemala, Paraguay, Charcas, Guemes, Malabia, Armenia, Pje. Virasoro, Gurruchaga, J. L. Borges, Thames, Gurruchaga, Uriarte, Darragueyra, Av. Santa Fe, Fray Justo de Santa María de Oro, Godoy Cruz

Palermo Viejo / Las Cañitas

Some of the several shops en El Salvador street.

Armenian Church.

Av. Cordoba

El Borde
Contemporary art.

Niceto Vega

Calma Chicha
Design objects.

Club and restaurant Ero's. It is an old neighborhood club where you can get good and inexpensive food.

Pte. Cabrer

Palermo paper shop,
papers and printings.

Pte. Soria

Plaza Cortázar

Pte. Sta. Rosa

Uriarte Space.
Contemporary art.

ussel

Ferrocarril Gral San Martin

Av. Juan B. Justo

La boutique del
Books, bar and shows.

Mott. Market cooking in El Salvador 1685. Minimalist and modern ambience.

Las Cañitas

View of the Islamic Center and the Mosque of King Fahd.

Near the argentine polo campus and the hippodrome between Libertador and Luis María Campos avenues we arrive to Las Cañitas neighborhood. It is a conglomerate of buildings and night restaurants, some of them of great quality. It is a very nosiy place during the night.

Very near this palce, in Bullrich and Libertador avenues we arrive to the Mosque and Islamic Center King Fahd, built by the government of Saudi Arabia. It is an enormous religious cultural and educative complex with its two huge minaret highlighting the neignorhood, that has changed its profile due to the real state market. Nowadays it is full of enormous and luxurious living towers that complete on their heights.

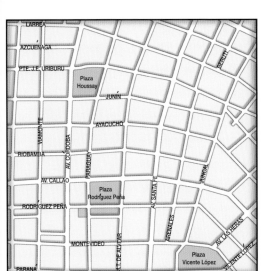

find a commercial area with movie theaters, bars, bookstores and restaurants that, together with Corrientes avenue, makes up the right location for the busiest nightlife in the city. On Saturdays night, this area is very attractive and buzzing with activity.

If we keep on moving towards downtown on Callao avenue, we will reach Rodriguez Peña Square and, on the background, we will see Pizurno Palace, current seat of the Ministry of Education. If we turn right on Córdoba avenue and walk one block in the same direction, we will get to Aguas Corrientes Palace, a clay building that has been richly decorated. Some steps further, we will find Houssay Square, which is bounded by the Economics College Building and the Medicine College Building and Hospital, which make up the biggest construction in the city. The small church in the middle of the square used to be the chapel of the old Learning Hospital, which was located on those premises. If we walk back to Callao avenue and we keep moving along it, we will get to Corrientes avenue.

If we go back downtown along Callao avenue, we will find a large residential area. A row of buildings with luxurious apartments stands on both sides of the avenue up to the spot where it reaches Santa Fe avenue. There we

Barrio Norte in 3 dimensions

The Medicine University Building covers the whole block and it is the biggest construction in the city. It was built in the 1930s.

Clinicas Hospital.

Houssay Square.

Economic Sciences University.

Tympanum of Economic Sciences University.

Clásica y Moderna is a very famous library, bar and restaurant.

Del Carmen church. Its big atrium contrasts with the small dimensions of the temple.

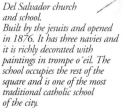

*Del Salvador church and school.
Built by the jesuits and opened in 1876. It has three navies and it is richly decorated with paintings in trompe o'eil. The school occupies the rest of the square and is one of the most traditional catholic school of the city.*

One of the most beautiful domes through Callao avenue. The picture is on the corner of Lavalle street.

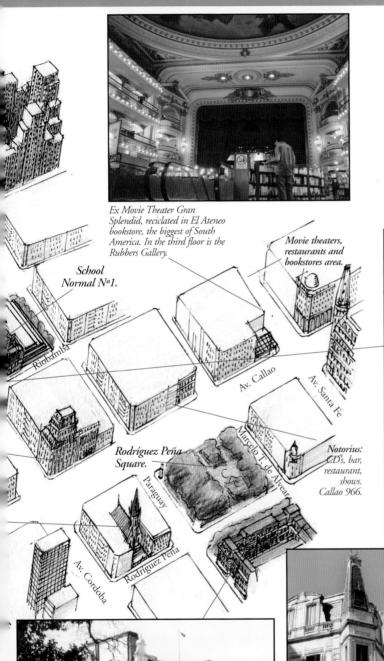

Ex Movie Theater Gran Splendid, reciclated in El Ateneo bookstore, the biggest of South America. In the third floor is the Rubbers Gallery.

School Normal Nº1.

Movie theaters, restaurants and bookstores area.

Riobamba

Av. Callao

Av. Santa Fe

Rodríguez Peña Square.

Marcelo T. de Alvear

Paraguay

Notorius: CD's, bar, restaurant, shows. Callao 966.

Av. Cordoba

Rodríguez Peña

Aguas Corrientes Palace: This gaudy building entirely decorated with English ceramic houses 12 water reservoirs, each of which can hold 70 million liters of water. Its strong outside walls are 1.80 meters thick. This palace, built in 1887, has been mentioned by Jorge Luis Borges in some of his stories, poems and essays.

Several Petit hotels are still standing in this area of the city.

Pizzurno Palace: it is the current seat of the Ministry of Education. It was designed in an elegant and harmonious French style and its walls bear an original bossage.

Obelisk in 3 dimensions

It was built in the 1930s by architect Prebich. It stands there to commemorate the place where the Argentinian flag was hoisted for the first time. The Church of St Nicholas used to be located on these plot of land and it was later moved to Santa Fe avenue, between Talcahuano and Uruguay streets.

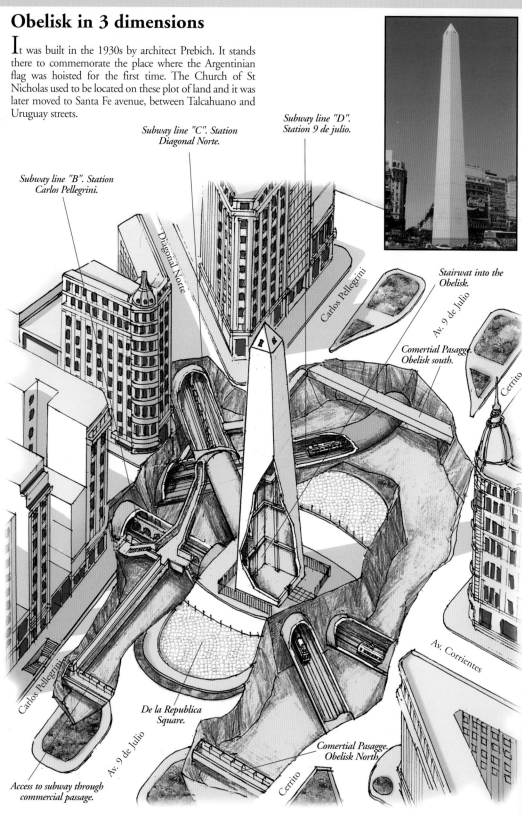

Subway line "C". Station Diagonal Norte.

Subway line "D". Station 9 de julio.

Subway line "B". Station Carlos Pellegrini.

Diagonal Norte

Carlos Pellegrini

Stairwat into the Obelisk.

Av. 9 de Julio

Comertial Pasagge. Obelisk south.

Cerrito

Cerrito

Av. Corrientes

Carlos Pellegrini

De la Republica Square.

Comertial Pasagge. Obelisk North.

Av. 9 de Julio

Cerrito

Access to subway through commercial passage.

Corrientes Avenue

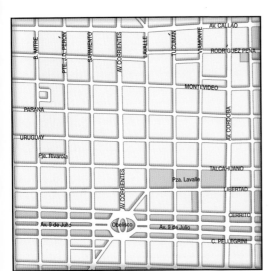

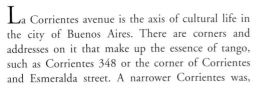

La Corrientes avenue is the axis of cultural life in the city of Buenos Aires. There are corners and addresses on it that make up the essence of tango, such as Corrientes 348 or the corner of Corrientes and Esmeralda street. A narrower Corrientes was, until the 1930s, the street where all tango celebrities used to gather. After the middle-1930s, it was widened and it became an avenue. It was only then that theaters and cinemas started to come up along it and it turned into the Argentinian Broadway. Undoubtedly, walking along Corrientes avenue in the evening is a must. A view of this avenue with the Obelisk on the background makes the typical postcard of Buenos Aires.

By the end of the 1950s, San Martín Theater and Cultural Center were built on Corrientes, which added another point of interest to the avenue. Theaters, cinemas, bars and libraries give it a bohemian and intellectual atmosphere. On next page, you will find a guide to the points of interest on Corrientes avenue.

Corrientes Avenue

Corrientes Avenue in 3 dimensions

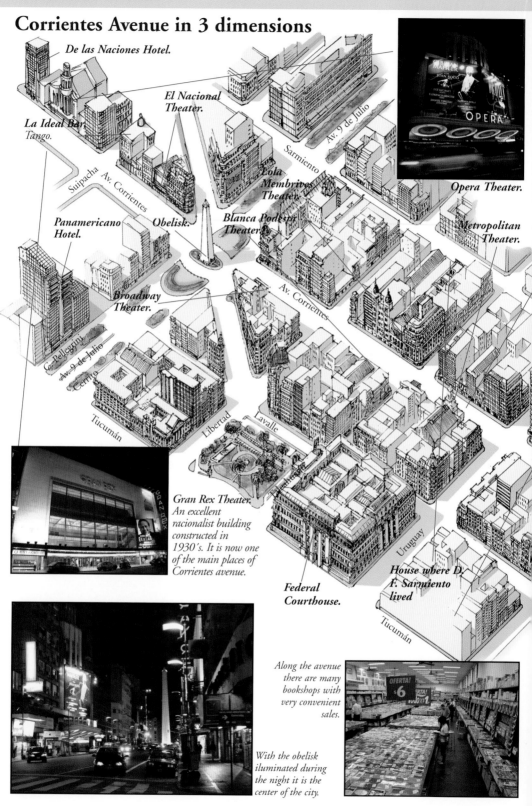

De las Naciones Hotel.

El Nacional Theater.

La Ideal Bar.
Tango.

Opera Theater.

Panamericano Hotel.

Obelisk.

Lola Membrives Theater.

Blanca Podestá Theater.

Metropolitan Theater.

Broadway Theater.

Gran Rex Theater.
An excellent racionalist building constructed in 1930's. It is now one of the main places of Corrientes avenue.

Federal Courthouse.

House where D. F. Sarmiento lived

Along the avenue there are many bookshops with very convenient sales.

With the obelisk iluminated during the night it is the center of the city.

La Paz: traditional bar and restaurant that serves as meeting point for artists and intellectuals, on the corner of Corrientes avenue and Montevideo street.

Guerrin Pizzeria. The most traditional.

La Giralda Bar.

San Martin Theater. *(see p. 106).*

Alvear Theater. *An excellent salon with a varied repertory, specially of prose theater and dancing.*

Cooperation Cultural Center
It is a modern art and cultural center. It houses a large auditorium and exhibition room. Many teaching activities also take place.

La Plaza Complex.
Theaters, bars and restaurants.

Lorca Cinema.
Emblematic room of independent cine, next to Leopoldo Lugones.

Sarmiento

Ramos Bar.

Los Angeles Cinema.
Especiallized in kids movies.

La Paz Bar.

Lavalle

Montevideo

Rodriguez Peña

Astral Theater.

Alvear Theater.

Gandhi Bookstore.

La Academia, another mythic bar. It is in Callao and corrientes avenues.

Av. Callao

Av. Corrientes

Riobamba

San Martín Theater and Cultural Center in 3 dimensiones

In 1960, the most modern and functional building of its time was opened in Buenos Aires. The huge complex had been designed by architect Mario Roberto Alvarez for the purpose of housing theaters, auditoriums, small movie projection rooms, etc.

The complex covers 29,350 square meters and both wings look clean and tidy at first sight, with enormous glass surfaces and powerful pillars that may be seen in the entrance hall.

It houses three theaters. The biggest one is called Martin Coronado and it can sit up to 1700 people. It is one of the newest and best-equipped halls in the city and its stage has witnessed the presence of the best local and international actors.

The Casacuberta theater is two stories below it, in the underground level, and it sits 560 people. It was designed as an amphitheater and it serves to put on plays that need more intimacy.

Across from the Casacuberta theater, in a spacious hall, you will find a huge mural painting 35 meters long and 11 meters high by Spanish artist Luis Seoane. It depicts theater pioneers in Argentina. On the 10th floor you will find Leopoldo Lugones hall, a small movie theater where artistic movies are usually projected.

The huge entrance hall usually serves as stage for free, world-class shows in the afternoon and evening.

The San martin theater has been joined to the San martin Cultural Center on Sarmiento avenue through a passage on the ground floor, where a photographs exhibition gallery directed by prestigious photographer Sara Facio is located.

In the entrance area of this gallery you will find a sculpture by Sesostris Vitullo called Martín Fierro.

The San Martin Cultural Center houses many exhibition rooms, a hall for experimental theater, an auditorium and an enormous convention hall. In the same building you will find the Tourism Department of the City of Buenos Aires, the Municipal Radio Station and a Conservatory of Music.

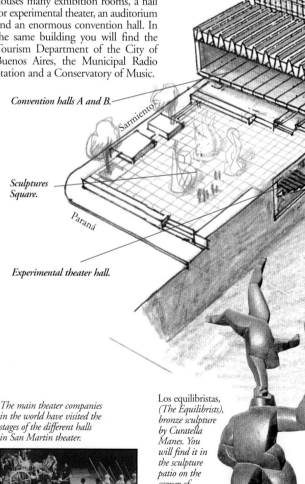

Municipal Radio Station.

Enrique Muiño Hall.

Convention halls A and B.

Sarmiento

Sculptures Square.

Paraná

Experimental theater hall.

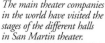

The main theater companies in the world have visited the stages of the different halls in San Martin theater.

Los equilibristas, (The Equilibrists), bronze sculpture by Curatella Manes. You will find it in the sculpture patio on the corner of Sarmiento and Paraná streets.

Corrientes Avenue

Teatro San Martín

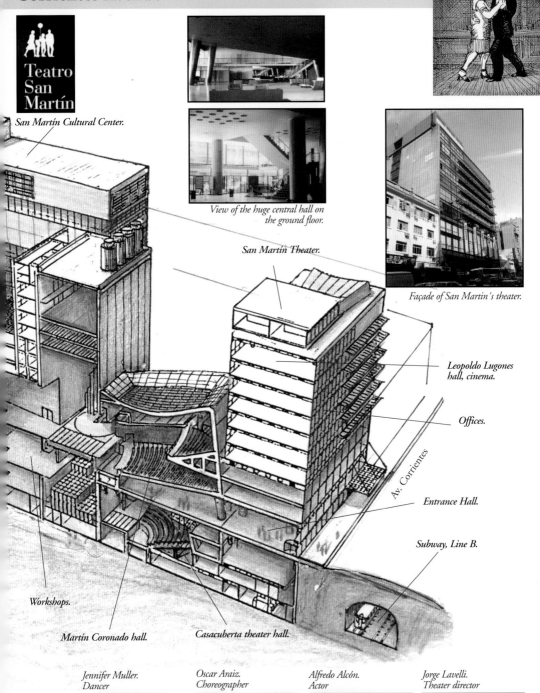

San Martín Cultural Center.

View of the huge central hall on the ground floor.

San Martín Theater.

Façade of San Martín's theater.

Leopoldo Lugones hall, cinema.

Offices.

Av. Corrientes

Entrance Hall.

Subway, Line B.

Workshops.

Martín Coronado hall.

Casacuberta theater hall.

Jennifer Muller.
Dancer

Oscar Araiz.
Choreographer

Alfredo Alcón.
Actor

Jorge Lavelli.
Theater director

EL PUEBLO
A
LAVALLE

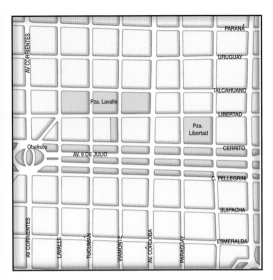

The mansion was demolished in 1937 in order to add those lands to the square, which thus covered the three blocks it still covers today. We suggest that you take a slow walk around the square and take your time to watch the sculptures and trees closely (see next page). Among the buildings whose facade looks upon the square, we should mention the Federal Courthouse, Roca School, the Colon Theater, Cervantes Theater and the Sinagogue of the Israeli Congregation in Argentina, where the square meets Tucumán street. In the middle of the square you will find a column with the statue of Juan Lavalle on top of it. The square has been named after him and he was a military man educated in San Martin's army. His life was pretty violent and he was the worst enemy of Dorrego's (governor of the province of Buenos Aires), a man he later had executed by shooting. Dorrego happened to be one of Felisa Dorrego's predecessors.

In 1840, Mariano Miró and Felisa Dorrego bought the lands where part of the square is located today and they built a huge mansion called Miró Palace, in the gardens of which they planted a collection of trees. Many of them still survive.

Plaza Lavalle in 3 dimensions

Cervantes Theater

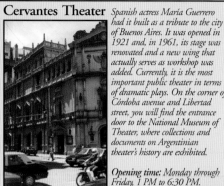

Spanish actress María Guerrero had it built as a tribute to the city of Buenos Aires. It was opened in 1921 and, in 1961, its stage was renovated and a new wing that actually serves as workshop was added. Currently, it is the most important public theater in terms of dramatic plays. On the corner of Córdoba avenue and Libertad street, you will find the entrance door to the National Museum of Theater, where collections and documents on Argentinian theater's history are exhibited.

Opening time: Monday through Friday, 1 PM to 6:30 PM.

Cervantes Theater in 3 dimensions

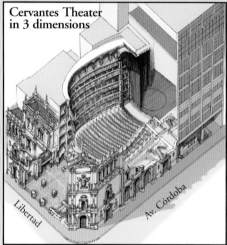

Libertad

Av. Córdoba

Massüe Balcony.
It is one of the few examples of Art Nouveau architecture in the city.

President Roca School: Greek-style building which has a magnificent façade with Ionic columns.

Colón Theater (see p. 112 to 115).
(see p. 112 to 115).

Ficus Macrofilia. *A tree whose trunk is over 80 meters in diameter.*

Carlos Pellegrini

Av. 9 de Julio

Cerrito

Libertad

Agatis Robusta. *tree of 150 years old*

Av. Córdoba

María Guerrero Garden.

Sinagogue of the Israeli Congregation in Argentina: Its looks upon Libertad street. The building dates from 1932 and it is one of the main synagogues in the city.

Plaza Lavalle

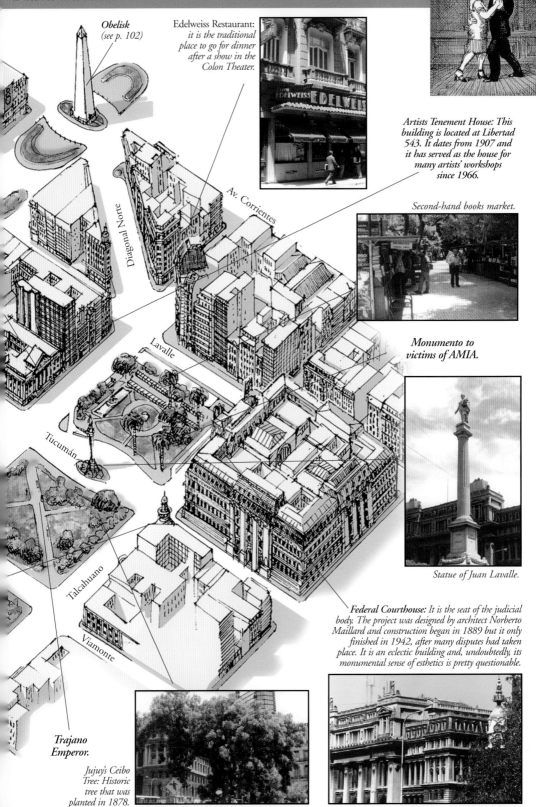

Obelisk
(see p. 102)

Edelweiss Restaurant:
it is the traditional
place to go for dinner
after a show in the
Colon Theater.

Av. Corrientes

Diagonal Norte

Artists Tenement House: This
building is located at Libertad
543. It dates from 1907 and
it has served as the house for
many artists' workshops
since 1966.

Second-hand books market.

Lavalle

**Monumento to
victims of AMIA.**

Tucumán

Talcahuano

Statue of Juan Lavalle.

Viamonte

Federal Courthouse: It is the seat of the judicial
body. The project was designed by architect Norberto
Maillard and construction began in 1889 but it only
finished in 1942, after many disputes had taken
place. It is an eclectic building and, undoubtedly, its
monumental sense of esthetics is pretty questionable.

**Trajano
Emperor.**

*Jujuy's Ceibo
Tree:* Historic
tree that was
planted in 1878.

111

Colón Theater in 3 dimensions

Façade of Colon Theater on Libertad street.

musical instruments. There is also a public library that has books on music and opera. If you go up any of the lateral stairs, you will get to the hall of Busts, a long wide corridor where you will find the faces of the most famous musicians of all times on the lintels. One of the lateral walks will take you to the Golden Hall, an exquisitely decorated room with gilded details and French furniture, chandeliers and vases. The main theater has an Italian-style horseshoe design, there are three stories with boxes on balconies, then a gallery for women, an upper gallery, another one above it and finally a paradise or top gallery. The theater is 33 meters in diameter and 28 meters high. The dome's ceiling was painted by famous artist Raúl Soldi. The main chandelier is a unique piece with more than 600 light bulbs. It weighs 2,500 kilos and a maximum of 20 people can stand inside of it to create sound effects during the show.

El The first building for the Colon Theater was located on Av de Mayo, where the National Bank stands today. By the end of the 19th Century, Buenos Aires had become a wealthy city and the theater was not as luxurious as the new generations wanted it to be, so the project for a new Colon Theater was designed. The original plans were drawn by Italian architect Francisco Tamburini and submitted for approval in 1829. The theater was to be located in front of Lavalle Square. After a series of never-ending difficulties, architect Julio Dormal finally finished it in 1908. The main theater has a seating capacity of 2,500 and it may accommodate up to 3,500 people if standing tickets are sold. The main entrance door to the orchestra floor and boxes is on Libertad street and the higher seating rows in the theater may be entered though the entrance doors on Toscanini and Tucumán streets.

The main hall is enormous and it is entirely covered in stucco that has been molded by Italian artisans. There is a combination of styles that may be appreciated by seeing the Ionic and Corinthian capitals. On the ceiling, there is a French stained-glass piece. The main staircase leading to the theater itself is made up of a combination of Carrara marbles from Verona and Portugal. The banister's tops are craved by a famous sculptor called Chapasco. In this hall you will find a small museum of history of the Colon Theater and a museum of old and valuable

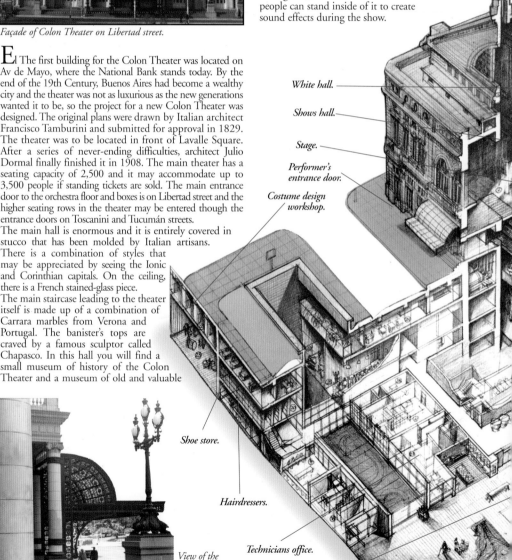

White hall.

Shows hall.

Stage.

Performer's entrance door.

Costume design workshop.

Shoe store.

Hairdressers.

Technicians office.

Scenography workshop.

View of the canopy built on the entrance door after the opening.

Plaza Lavalle

View of the upper galleries as seen from the entrance hall.

Theater with dome's ceiling painted by Raúl Soldi and main chandelier with over 600 light bulbs.

Main Hall.

Golden Hall.

Entrance for visitors.

Guided tours: *Monday through Friday: 9 AM, 10 AM, 11 AM, 12 AM, 1 PM, 2 PM, 3 PM and 4 PM. Saturdays: : 9 AM, 10 AM, 11 AM and 12 AM.*
Admission: $ 5.
Toscanini street 1180.
Information: 4382-6632.

Storage Rooms.

Hall of Busts.

Dance hall.

Scenography workshop.

Balconies with caryatids on the façade upon Libertad street.

Machinery and Carpenter's workshop.

Stage designers workshop on the third underground level.

Sculpture workshop.

Front on Arturo Toscanini street. Pilasters and low relieves of italian style.

Colon Theater, workshops and artistic bodies

Rehearsal hall in 9 de Julio street, located on the third underground.

Construction of monumental sculpture for "Turandot".

The theater's workshops are located in the underground levels. It is one of the few opera houses in the world in which most of the articles needed for the show may be produced. It has a stage designers workshop, a hairdresser's, a shoemaking workshop, a costume design workshop, a carpenter's workshop, etc.

Quite an army of people work in these underground levels, which stretch below Viamonte street and 9 de Julio avenue.

The Colon Theater has its own art companies: a Philharmonic Orchestra, a Choir and a Ballet Company. There are over one hundred company members in all.

The main opera and ballet starts in the world have set foot on the theater's stage, among them we can mention: Lili Pons, Enrique Caruso, María Callas and Luciano Pavarotti (the most famous opera singers in this century)

Scenography workshop on the third subfloor.

as well as Rudolf Nureyev and Nijinsky (the main ballet dancers). Julio Boca, Maximiliano Herrera and Paloma Herrera, the most important ballet dancers from Argentina, were educated in the Colon Theater's school.

Among musicians and conductors, we should mention the performance of Richard Strauss in 1920, as well as the concerts given by Igor Stravinsky and the unforgettable shows of Pablo Casals and Manuel de Falla. Arturo Toscanini conducted the theater's orchestra in many opportunities and it is in his honor that one of the lateral streets of the theater has been called Toscanini.

The list of famous performers is never-ending, but we could also mention the Vienna Boys' Choir, Alfredo Kraus, José Carreras, Plácido Domingo, Herbert Von Karajian, Maurice Bejart, Margot Fontaine, Maia Plissetskaya, etc.

Marcia Haydee and the struttgart ballet.

Scene of Les Sylphides.

Scenography storage.

Astor Piazzolla: he gave his consecrating concert in the theater.

Richard Strauss conducted in the Colon Theater during his two visits to Buenos Aires.

Beniamino Gigli performed in the theater many seasons.

Mascagni conducted his Cavalleria rusticana in 1911.

The Great Domes

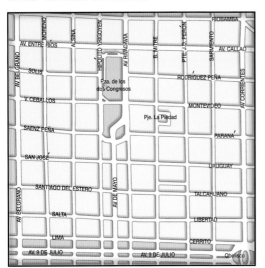

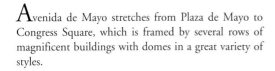

Avenida de Mayo stretches from Plaza de Mayo to Congress Square, which is framed by several rows of magnificent buildings with domes in a great variety of styles.

The most outstanding ones are the Barolo building, the Inmobiliaria building, the Urban Heritage building, the Molino building and the National Congress building.

Congress Square was created to commemorate the centennial of the May Revolution in 1910 and it was designed as a monumental frame for the Congress building, which had been opened in 1906.

In the square, the Fountain of the Two Congresses stands out with its huge staircases and banisters. At dusk, the combination of water, music and lights makes up a nice show.

On the corner of Bartolomé Mitre and Paraná streets you will find the Church of la Piedad, a spacious example of neoclassical architecture. That block on Bartolomé Mitre street is another one among the many Parisian corners in the city. In La piedad Passage you will find restaurants and nightclubs.

Plaza Congreso in 3 dimensions

The area is full of cafés and bars with tables on the sidewalk, and there are also some theaters and nightclubs. The most important theater among them is Avenida Theater, a traditional house where zarzuelas (Spanish form of light opera) are usually performed. A group of excellent Spanish restaurants surrounds the theater. Across the street from the square, on Rivadavia street, you will see Liceo Theater, a traditional old little theater.

The Avila Bar on Av de Mayo 1300 and Agua y Fuego on Rivadavia 1400 are nice places to have dinner in and enjoy Flamenco shows at the same time.

Former Magestic hotel, square dome. (see p. 122).

Dome of the building next to the National Senate, located in Alsina street and Entre Ríos avenue.

Photos: Otilio Moralejo.

Pinacle of the dome of La Inmobiliaria building. (see p. 122).

Statue to the Thinking man by Auguste Rodin.

El Imparcial restaurant. Spanish food. Salta 97.

El Globo restaurant. Spanish food. Salta 98.

Avenida Theater.

San José

Santiago del Estero

Hipolito Yrigoyen

Salta

Lima

Libertad

Rivadavia

Av. de Mayo

Castelar Hotel.

Cerrito

Hispano restaurant. Spanish food. Salta 26.

Dome of Urban Heritage Building, located in Rivadavia avenue and Paraná street.

Av. 9 de Julio

LA CUEVA bookstore. Av. de Mayo 1119.

Plaza Congreso and surrounding area

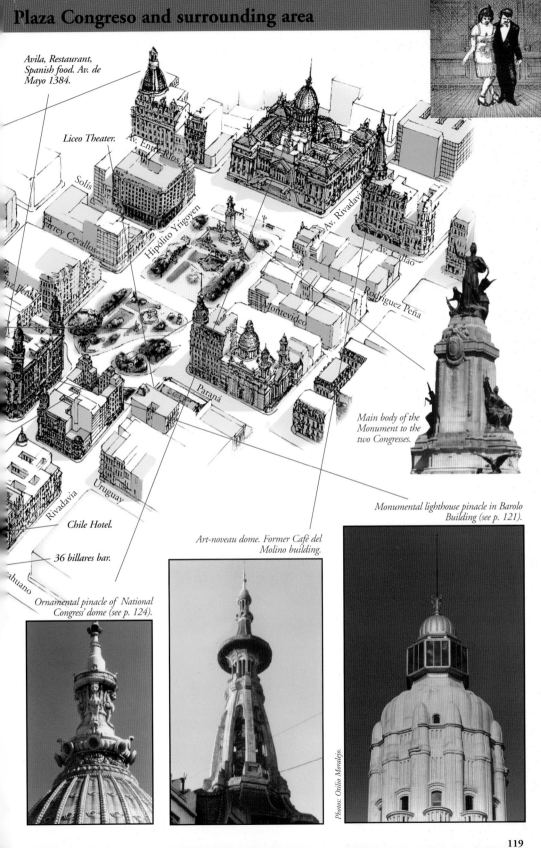

Avila, Restaurant, Spanish food. Av. de Mayo 1384.

Liceo Theater.

Av. Entre Ríos.

Solís

Virrey Cevallos

Hipólito Yrigoyen

Saenz Peña

Av. Rivadavia

Av. Callao

Rodríguez Peña

Montevideo

Paraná

Rivadavia

Uruguay

Chile Hotel.

36 billares bar.

Catamarca

Main body of the Monument to the two Congresses.

Monumental lighthouse pinacle in Barolo Building (see p. 121).

Ornamental pinacle of National Congress' dome (see p. 124).

Art-noveau dome. Former Café del Molino building.

Photos: Otilia Moralejo.

119

Barolo Building

The successive curve and straight lines of balconies and cornices convey a dramatic style to the tower.

Metallic structure where the revolving lighthouse is placed.

It dates from 1922 and it was designed by Italian architect Mario Palanti. For a period, it was the highest building in Buenos Aires. A rare example of expressionist architecture, it has a monumental appearance and a spacious gallery that reaches Hipólito Irigoyen street. Even though this gallery is somehow deteriorated, it is still faithful to its original appearance. If you take a close look at the building, you will find some hidden esoteric details included by architect Palanti, such as the gargoyles, the dragons, the circles and the balustrades that may be seen in the main vault.

The number and measures of these elements have been taken from figures and keys provided by Dante in The Divine Comedy.

Photos: Otilio Moralejo

The perspective on Av. de Mayo makes Barolo building look as one of the most outstanding buildings in the city.

Access to offices.

Dome of the gallery where the access to stairs and lifts is located.

The circle balustrades in the central dome are one of the many hidden details extracted from the Divine Comedy.

Gallery to Hipólito Irigoyen street.

La Inmobiliaria Building

Constructed by the insurance company with that name in 1910, is a mixture of styles. The 1st floor with statues, arcades and balconies are definetely italian. The two big domes on the corners give it an original, exotic and oriental touch.

Balcony on the second floor imitating a renacentist loggia.

Embossed metal pinacle completing the corner domes.

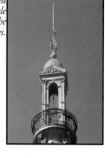

Pte. Luis Sáenz Peña

San José

Av. de Mayo

Former *Crítica* Newspaper

Built by architect Kalnay. It is a strange example of art-deco architecture and expressionist elements. It is located on the 1300 of Av. De Mayo.

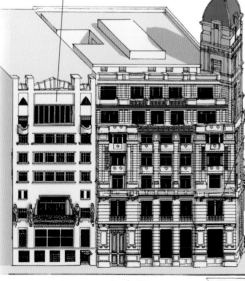

Av. de Mayo

Former Majestic Hotel

It serves as headquarters for a government office nowadays but it used to be one of the main hotels in the city. Its robust frame has a square dome on top of it. This is the place where Nijinsky resided during his stay in Buenos Aires.

Chile Hotel

A solid frame with art-noveau decoration. The corner balcony was completed by a onion-shaped dome conveying an oriental-style to its lines. It is located in 1400 Av. de Mayo.

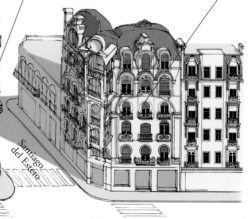

Santiago del Estero

Avenida Theater

(Av. De Mayo 1222) It was recently restored after a fire. It is

Hall designed as a horse shoe in diagonal to Avenida de Mayo.

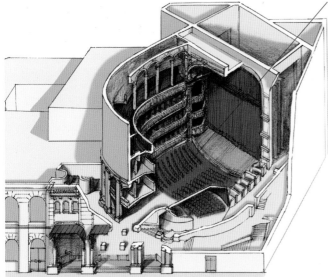

Av. de Mayo

Avenida Theater façade.

Neoclassical-style pinacle of La Piedad church's bell tower.

De la Piedad Church

This church was designed in a typical neoclassical style with a huge central nave and a high dome. The church is richly decorated on the inside and it has icons that date from the 18th Century.

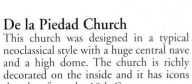

Inside of the church with decorative paintings in the whole surface.

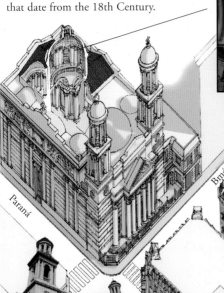

Paraná

Bmé. Mitre

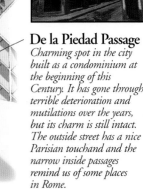

De la Piedad Passage

Charming spot in the city built as a condominium at the beginning of this Century. It has gone through terrible deterioration and mutilations over the years, but its charm is still intact. The outside street has a nice Parisian touchand the narrow inside passages remind us of some places in Rome.

El Tumi. Restaurant, Peruvian food.

National Congress in 3 dimensions

Photo: Otilio Moralejo.

The huge central dome of the National Congress building is meant to remind us of its sister in Washington. The building bears some perfectly carved caryatids, quadrigas and capitals you should not miss. Inside of it, there is a series of beautiful halls and a library with a wide range of valuable and out of print books. It houses the two chambers that make up Argentina's legislative body: the Chamber of

Under a law enacted in 1889, the National Congress was moved to the lands of an old sawmill on the block bound by Callao street, Hipólito Irigoyen street, Pozos street and Rivadavia avenue. In 1896, once Av de Mayo had been finished, the government opened an international bidding for the building's construction works. As a result of this process, construction of the building was left in the hands of architect Victor Meano, who had been working in the country for a while and helping architect Tamburini in the Colon Theater project and other buildings.

The National Congress is a monumental building in a classic Greek-Latin style. It may be viewed properly from Av de Mayo, which makes up an axis with the Executive Office Building or Pink House on one end and the National

Hipólito Yrigoyen

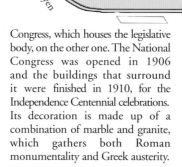

Congress, which houses the legislative body, on the other one. The National Congress was opened in 1906 and the buildings that surround it were finished in 1910, for the Independence Centennial celebrations. Its decoration is made up of a combination of marble and granite, which gathers both Roman monumentality and Greek austerity.

Representatives covers the back central area of the building and its semicircular shape may be seen from Pozos street, where as the Chamber of Senators is located in the left wing of the building and it is quite smaller. Undoubtedly, the most magnificent spot in the building is the Blue Hall, which lies under the big dome (approx. 60 meters high). The ceiling

View of the congress as seen from Avenida de Mayo.

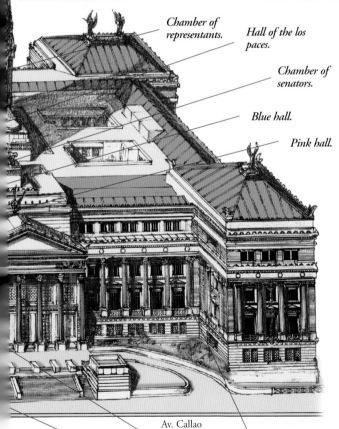

Chamber of representants.

Hall of the los paces.

Chamber of senators.

Blue hall.

Pink hall.

Av. Callao

Reading hall of the chamber of senators.

Big hall.

Caryatids at the National Congress'side door.

Library.

bears some beautiful marble cravings, some allegoric statues and a 2-ton chandelier made up of bronze and Baccarat crystal.In this place, the funeral honors of the most principal politicians are held.

Nowadays, the building is insufficient due to the increasing of the burocracy, that´s why many of the large buildings are annexed to it.

Greek Roman style decoration.

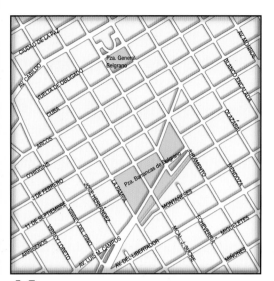

N orth of Palermo, if you walk along Cabildo or Luis María Campos avenues, you will reach Belgrano neighborhood.

Subway line "D" also reaches Belgrano's commercial area, above Juramento station.

Near middle 19th Century, Belgrano was a settlement apart from the City of Buenos Aires; in 1880, it became the seat of the National Government due to political circumstances. It was in said year that Belgrano was made a city on its own, but in the 1890s it had already become part of the capital city.

The historic area surrounds General Manuel Belgrano square, where you may find a crafts market on Saturdays and Sundays. Across from the square, on the corner of Juramento avenue and Vuelta de Obligado street, you will find the Museum of Sapnish Art "Enrique Larreta". The neocolonial building was erected in 1916 and it was home to writer Enrique Larreta.

In front of the square, near Arcos street, you will also find "Sarmiento Museum", which was seat to the National Government in 1880. It has been open since 1938 as a museum devoted to former President Domingo Faustino Sarmiento.

Photo: Otilio Moralejo.

Belgrano in 3 dimensions

Photo: Otilio Moralejo.

View of the Inmaculada Concepción Church, also known as "La Redonda". Its dome can be seen above the dense vegetation that surrounds it.

Subway station Juramento, line D.

Sarmiento History Museum
Cuba 2079.
Tours: *thursday to Sunday from 15 PM to 19 PM*

Metalic gazebo located in Barrancas de Belgrano park.

Undoubtely, the most outstanding building that you can see from the square is the Inmaculada Concepción Church, also known as "La Redonda" (the Round Church), which was opened in 1878. The main body of this unusual church is round and it is framed by two symmetrical shelters.

Until mid 20th. Century, the area was characterized by huge houses and tree-lined streets and avenues. Nowadays, the trees have become green domes that protect walkers from the sun and make it extremely pleasant to walk along those streets in the summer.

The high rise apartment buildings that have recently been erected (most of which are higher than 30 floors), together with the old mansions provide a modern and, at the same time, traditional profile to the neighborhood.

The main commercial areas in the neighborhood are located along most of Cabildo avenue and Juramento avenue, between Cabildo and Barrancas de Belgrano.

Barrancas de Belgrano is the most important green area in the neighborhood. It is a huge park surrounded by enormous modern-style buildings. Among these buildings, you will find the "Libero Badii Museum", an old mansion devoted to the work of the Italian sculpture and painter it is named after.

The park was redesigned in 1892 by landscape designer Carlos Thays. Barrancas de Belgrano is plenty of miradors and terraces, and it also has a wonderful metalic gazebo. Among the numerous plants and trees that can be found in the park, you may see centennial magnolias. A scale reproduction of New York's Statue of Liberty stands among the trees.

If you walk five blocks from Barrancas de Belgrano, along Luis María Campos avenue, you will reach "El Solar de la Abadía" shopping mall. Both the mall and its surroundings are among the most sophisticated and exclusive areas of the city. There, we will find excellent restaurants.

Mirador localted on Sucre street in Barrancas de Belgrano park. It provides an excellent view of the surrounding area.

Rogelio Yrurtia Museum.

Façade of the Rogelio Yrurtia Museum. O'Higgins 2390 Opened wednesday to friday from 3 to 7.30 PM. Saturday from 4 to 8 PM.

Líbero Badii Museum.

Descendimiento (Descent). Polychrome wood carving, 17th. Century

China Town

If you cross Virrey Vertiz avenue and the railways through Belgrano station, you will find "China Town", which is located along Arribeños, Montañeses, Mendoza and Juramento streets. There is plenty of Chinese restaurants, grocery stores and shops selling imported goods from the East. There are also some Buddhist temples and a monastery.

Barrancas de Belgrano

Mendoza

Juramento

O'Higgins

Zavalia

Echeverría

Sucre

Virrey Vértiz

Belgrano C Station, Mitre station.

Arribeños

Mendoza

Juramento

Montañeses

Museum of Spanish Art Enrique Larreta

It is a museum devoted to Spanish art. It features works that date from 13th. to 20th. Centuries, such as colorful carvings and altarpieces. The building represents the style of early 20th. Century mansions in Belgrano neighborhood. Its large Andalusian garden with Moorish fountains is unique.

Opening time: *From 3 to 8 PM. Monday and Wednesday closed.*
Guided tours: *Sunday at 4 and 6 PM.*
Admission: *$1. Thurdays free.*
Juramento 2291. Tel: 4784-4040

View of one of the museum's hall.

Argentine Museum of Natural Sciences
Bernardino Rivadavia

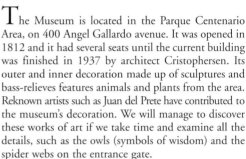

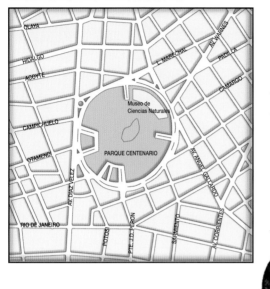

The Museum is located in the Parque Centenario Area, on 400 Angel Gallardo avenue. It was opened in 1812 and it had several seats until the current building was finished in 1937 by architect Cristophersen. Its outer and inner decoration made up of sculptures and bass-relieves features animals and plants from the area. Reknown artists such as Juan del Prete have contributed to the museum's decoration. We will manage to discover these works of art if we take time and examine all the details, such as the owls (symbols of wisdom) and the spider webs on the entrance gate.

In the entrance hall, you will find huge metalic meteors that were found in Argentina. You may visit a large hall containing a collection of minerals and scale reproductions of the surface of the Earth.

To the left of the entrance hall, there is a small aquarium with exotic species and an area with a complete collection of shells.

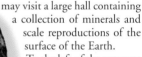

Museum of Natural Sciences

Undoubtedly, the most interesting part of the museum is the Paleontology Hall, probably the most important of its kind in Latin America. When you visit the hall, you will see many dinosaurs that have been found in Argentina by the museum's research teams. Among them, there are Carnotaurs and Glyptodonts, prehistoric inhabitants of the area now covered by the City of Buenos Aires.

On the first floor, there is a Compared Anatomy area and a large hall of birds, where we can appreciate a wide variety of South American species, many of which are placed in dioramas that reproduce their natural habitat.

One of the wings on the first floor is full of whales bones and other marine mammals' skeletons.

Last but not least, the arthropods hall contains several collections displayed in windows following didactic criteria.

Arthropodos.

View of the Paleontology Hall, dinosaurs found in Argentina on the foreground.

Address: Angel Gallardo 490.
Opening time: Monday through Sunday from 2 PM to 7 PM.
Admission: $1.
Guided tours: Tuesdays and Thursdays 10 AM
(English and French requests at 4982-4494).

Ostriches and deers in the Pampa pastures.

PASTIZAL PAMPEANO

Photo: Otilio Moralejo

The museum has got various kinds of carnotaurs, like the one in the picture.

Museum of Natural Sciences

Glyptodont: the natural habitat of this species was the Pampa planes. Some of them have been found on excavations in the area of the City of Buenos Aires.

Cetacea and mammals hall in the first floor of the museum.

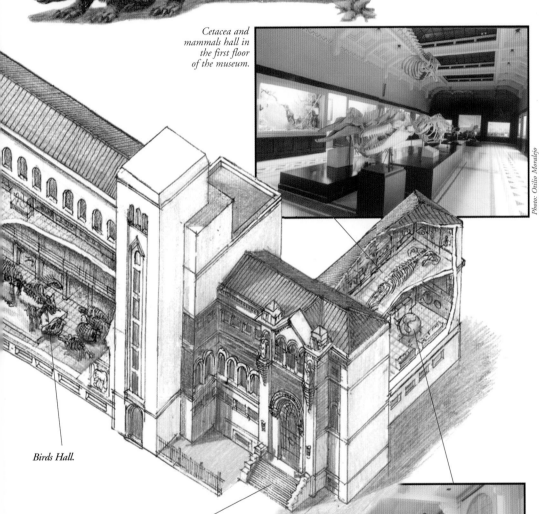

Photo: Otilia Moralejo

Birds Hall.

Main entrance.

Geology and Minerology Hall, infront of the entrance.

El Abasto

In 1890, a foodstuffs market called Abasto was erected on Corrientes avenue. Some time later, a new neighborhood started to grow around it and it took the market's name. In 1931, construction works began for a new market building in modernist Art-decó style with big domes in reinforced concrete.

In the early 20th Century, when the first market was built, the area took a different shape thanks to the presence of carriages, laborers, hostels and canteens which gave it a marginal ambience where tango music, popular songs and people's poetry were easily spread. One of the most important tango figures that lived in the area was Carlos Gardel, the city's mythical singer. Today, a street and a subway station that carry his name remind us of his presence in the neighborhood. The area is taking new shape again now: high-rise apartment buildings, five-star hotels, night clubs and theaters are being built and the old market has become a giant shopping mall.

View of the old market in the 1930s.

Zelaya street and its surrounding was decorated by the painter Mariano Santamarina with colourful portraits of Gardel and musical scores.

El Abasto

Abasto is the emblamatic place of tango; Gardel lived and sang there and it was also visited by Anibal Troilo and Osvaldo Pugliese, among others.

The museum-house of Carlos Gardel is an obliged visit such as Troilo´s house (the "bandoneón" of the tango) that was born in 1914 at 2937 of Cabrera street.

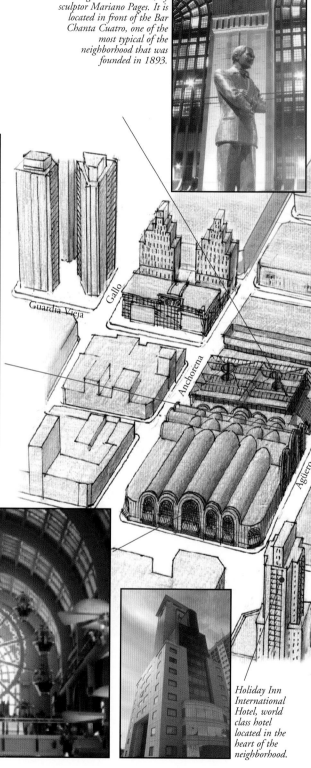

Monument to mythical singer Carlos Gardel, by sculptor Mariano Pages. It is located in front of the Bar Chanta Cuatro, one of the most typical of the neighborhood that was founded in 1893.

Guardia Vieja

Gallo

Anchorena

Agüero

Details of the monumental archery.

Interior of the restored building where a big shopping mall stands today.

Holiday Inn International Hotel, world class hotel located in the heart of the neighborhood.

El Abasto

Museum Carlos Gardel's House.
735 Jean Jaures street. Carlos Gardel bought this house in 1926 and lived there with his mother Berthe Gardel till 1933. That is why he was called El Morocho de Abasto. The house contains personal remembrances and an important photographic documentation.

Zelaya

Lavalle

Jean Jaurés

los Gardel

Av. Corrientes

Filet Passage.
700 Jean Jaures street.
The filet is a traditional way of decorative painting brought from Italy and developed in Buenos Aires in the popular suburbs. That is why the esthetic is linked to the tango. It was mainly used in Abasto to decorate carts and later, trucks and buses. In this area there are façades that homage esthetic.

The Argentine tango and its characteristics

The origins of tango music date back to the period that stretches from the 1850s to the 1880s. Tango music is deeply influenced by African-American rhythms, such as candombe and habanera, and by some European dances, such as Spanish contredanse and the so-called Andalusian tango. Those are the predecessors of Argentinian tango.

In the late 19th Century, the so-called suburban tango became consolidated. At the beginning, people used to dance the tango in the suburbs and it was not until the early 20th Century that it was accepted as a decent dance in luxurious downtown dance halls.

Tango music later took its strength of character and melancholy cadence from the mainly Italian and Spanish immigrants that arrived in the city at the begining of this Century. Around 1910, tango music had already spread to Europe and it was widely accepted in all the big cities in the world, whereas in Buenos Aires it still aroused suspicion, specially among members of the Catholic Church, who even condemned it.

Hansen's, the Armenonville and Chanteclair were the places where this dance was first accepted and their customers quickly became fans of it. Dance parties and

Narrow Corrientes street.

meetings started to spread all around the city at a fast pace and thus appeared the greatest tango composers, performers, dancers and writers in the city. At this stage, the bandoneon became the main musical instrument in Typical Orchestras, that is, tango orchestras created by Vicente Greco. In the 1920s, tango music became worldwide famous and Buenos Aires, which was enjoying good economical conditions at the time, showed itself as the Queen of the River Plate. Its nightlife gained fame together with Corrientes street (which had not become an avenue yet) and its huge cabarets.

This situation lead tango music to its golden period. The most important figure in tango music is Carlos Gardel, a mythical singer born in France and raised in the Abasto market neighborhood, who possessed a great deal of magnetism and a privileged voice. Carlos Gardel was responsible for taking tango music to Broadway and Hollywood.

Vicente Greco.

Carlos Gardel with the so-called New York Blondes: he embodies the myth of the Argentine winner who attains success in Hollywood.

The protagonists

Agustín Bardi, Julio Decaro, Celedonio Flores, Discépolo, Osvaldo Fresedo, Osvaldo Pugliese and Aníbal Troilo were the main tango composers and performers in Argentina. In the 1920-1950 period several tango schools were created: some of them supported sung tango and focused on the poetics of the lyrics, whereas others, such as that of Anibal Troilo or Osvaldo Pugliese, supported the dance side of tango. Among great tango singers we should mention Julio Sosa, Edmundo Rivero, Roberto Goyeneche, Libertad Lamarque and Hugo del Carril. Tango lyrics writers were great poets, as is the case with Homero Manzi, Horacio Ferrer, and even Jorge Luis Borges himself, who did not miss the chance to write the lyrics of some famous tango songs.

Astor Piazzolla, a musician and disciple of Anibal Troilo, was also the last great innovator in tango music. He placed it closer to contemporary music and was widely accepted and acknowledged as one of the greatest composers of these times. Nowadays, thousands of tourist arrive in Buenos Aires with a main goal: watching tango shows and learning how to dance to the beat of this fascinating music that is, as a great poet once said, "a sad feeling you can dance to".

Francisco Canaro's Tango Orchestra.

Homero Manzi.
Poet.

Aníbal Troilo "Pichuco".
Musician and Composer.

Julio Sosa.
Singer.

Carlos Gardel.
Singer.

Osvaldo Fresedo.
Composer.

El Polaco Goyeneche.
Singer.

Astor Piazzolla.
Musician and Composer.

Clothing

After some time, the tango also introduced a traditional attire: a wide-brimmed hat, a cut in the skirt, and a particular kind of shoe indispensable for tango partners.

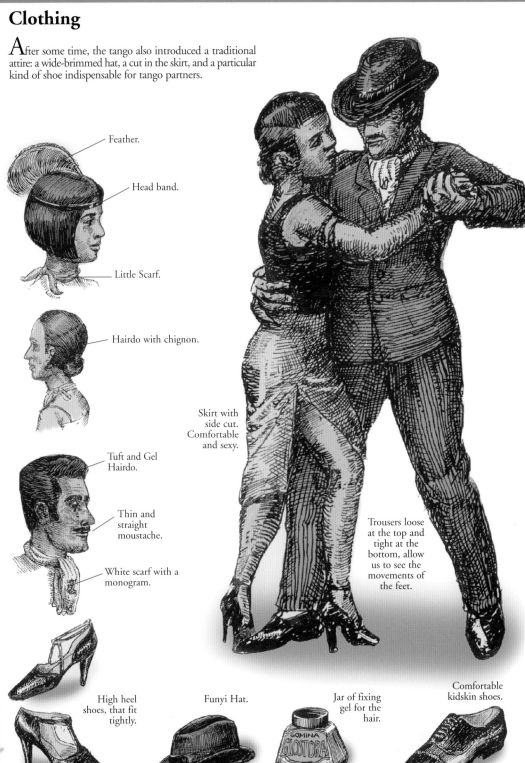

Feather.

Head band.

Little Scarf.

Hairdo with chignon.

Tuft and Gel Hairdo.

Thin and straight moustache.

White scarf with a monogram.

Skirt with side cut. Comfortable and sexy.

Trousers loose at the top and tight at the bottom, allow us to see the movements of the feet.

Comfortable kidskin shoes.

High heel shoes, that fit tightly.

Funyi Hat.

Jar of fixing gel for the hair.

The tango

These drawings show some of the relevant steps of the most famous dance in Buenos Aires. The style shown here is the Ballroom Tango of the twenties. It's an intimate dance of controlled eroticism far from the spectacular acrobatics, jumps, and contortions done basically in the Tango for export.

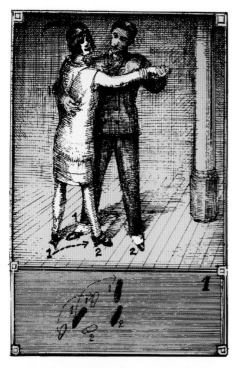

Double swinging sit: The man's right foot moves back till it reaches the same level of his left foot and meets the woman's left foot.

The Sit: The man's left foot makes a slight curve and the woman's right foot moves back forming a large curve.

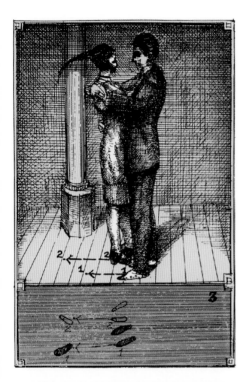

The Exit: The man moves forward with his left foot and the woman moves back with her right foot.

The Double Step: The right leg crosses behind the left leg, it follows the direction of the arrow till the second "1" and moves back till the final position of the arrow at the third "1".

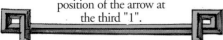

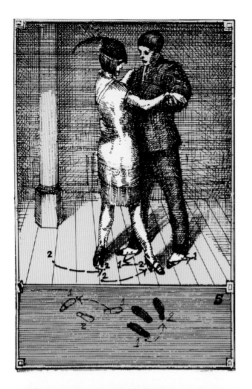

"It is not a matter of being friends while dancing. The secret lies in a silence's sheath that makes us taciturn, almost resentful".
Juan Carlos Lamadrid

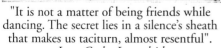

Buenos Aires, world´s capital of tango

Since some years ago, the city organizes festivals and championships of tango that are very popular not only in the provinces but also we have a great presence of people from outside. This call is concentrated in three main events that will be described.

VII Buenos Aires Tango Festival:
From February 23rd to march 4th, 2007
Leading figures and new talents. The classic, the innovative, the crossover.
Concerts outdoors at theatres, at cultural centres and at historic bars.
Concerts outdoors, at theaters, at cultural centers and at historic bars.
Dance lessons, film, milongas and exhibitions.
Music, poetry, dance, art…
The entire tango culture vibrates year after year at the Buenos Aires Tango Festival.

IV Tango Dance Metropolitan Championship:
May and June 2007
Every night Buenos Aires milongas are filled with couples reinventing the most genuine, popular way of dancing tango.
Every year, the best dancers gather at the Tango Dance Metropolitan Championship to vindicate their status as milongueros and crown the winners, who are to represent Buenos Aires at the World Championship.
The Championship, a tournament for experts. And a unique chance to enjoy the magic of the milonga party.

IV Tango Dance World Championship:
From 17th to 27th August 2007
Today Tango is danced across the world. And the whole world is anxious to dance tango in Buenos Aires.
So, the Tango Dance World Championship will summon the world´s top dancers. The competition, divided into two categories, gives room to the popular culture (Salon Tango), two sides of a dance that enamors multitudes without distinction of nationality.
No matter where you are, if you can dance, you could become the World Champion in the Tango Capital of the world.

Information
www.tangodata.gov.ar
Te.: +54 11 4374-2829
Toll-free line only for Argentina: 0800-3-337848
Mondays thru Fridays 11 am to 7 pm.

Information given by: Buenos Aires Government. Culture Ministry.

Tanguerías – tango shows – dinners

Buenos Aires nights are full of milongas This popular dance is practiced not only by porteños but also by tourists who come to learn this sensual and different dance. Bailongos and milongas are distributed along the city. Some with a certain touristic and commercial characteristic and the most recommended are the ones that conserve the real porteño spirit.

Through Corrientes avenue we will find shows dedicated to the tango of great quality thought for tourists.

A Media Luz (San Telmo)
Chile 316
Tel.: 4331-6146/1872

Armenonville (Recoleta)
Alvear 1879
Tel.: 4804-1033/4033

Bar Sur (San Telmo)
Estados Unidos 299
Tel.: 4362-6086

Casa Blanca (San Telmo)
Balcarce 668
Tel.: 4331-4621/4343-5002

Claroscuro (San Telmo)
Balcarce 971
Tel.: 4300-2816/8918

El Querandí (Monserrat)
Perú 302 esq. Moreno
Tel.: 4345-0331/1770

El Viejo Almacén (San Telmo)
Independencia y Balcarce
Tel.: 4307-7388

La Cumparsita (San Telmo)
Chile 302 esq. Balcarce
Tel.: 4361-6880

La Ventana (Monserrat)
Balcarce 425
Tel.: 4331-0217

Michelángelo (Monserrat)
Balcarce 433
Tel.: 4328-2646

Sabor a Tango (Barracas)
Av. Belgrano 2378
Tel.: 4942-2591

Señor Tango (Balvanera)
Vieytes 1655
Tel.: 4303-0231/34

Tangoteca (Puerto Madero)
Alicia Moreau de Justo 1728
Tel.: 4311-1988

Centro Cultural Torcuato Tasso
Defensa 1575 (San Telmo)
Tel.: 4307-6506

Noches de 2 x 4
Nights of 2 x 4
bailes - shows

Esquina Carlos Gardel (Abasto)
Carlos Gardel 3200
Tel.: 4867-6363

Esquina Homero Manzi (Boedo)
Av. San Juan 360
Tel.: 4857-8488

Café Bar Bajo San Telmo
(San Telmo)
San Lorenzo 365
Tel.: 4362-0537

Buenos Aires Sur
(Barracas)
Villarino 2359
Tel.: 4301-6758

Café Homero (Palermo)
Cabrera 4946
Tel.: 4773-1979

Caminito Tango Show (La Boca)
Del Valle Iberlucea 1151
Tel.: 4301-1520

Club del Vino (Palermo)
Cabrera 4737 - Tel.: 4833-0050

Club Villa Modelo (Villa Urquiza)
Arismendi 2684 esq. Ávalos

El Chino (Pompeya)
Beazley 3566 - Tel.: 4911-0215

Kafetín (San Cristóbal)
Av. Independencia 2200
Tel.: 4308-2055

Clases de tango
Tango lessons

Círculo Bailable de la Armada
(Caballito)
José María Moreno 355
Tel.: 4903-6531

Club Almagro (Almagro)
Medrano 522
Tel.: 4774-7454

Confitería La Ideal (San Nicolás)
Suipacha 384 1°
Tel.: 4605-8234

La Galería (Caballito)
Boedo 722
Tel.: 4957-1829

Nuevo Salón La Argentina (Balvanera)
Bartolomé Mitre 1759

Acordes de Tango (San Telmo)
Humberto 1° 873
Tel.: 4307-5474

Centro Cultural Gral. San Martín
(San Nicolás)
Sarmiento 1551 piso 2, sala 14

La Escuela de Tango (Monserrat)
San José 364 3°
Tel.: 4383-0466

Morocco (Balvanera)
Corrientes 2048
Tel.: 4954-6911/2

Spell Café (Puerto Madero)
Alicia Moreau de Justo 740
Tel.: 4334-0512

Escuela Argentina de Tango
Centro Cultural Borges
Viamonte y San Martín
Tel.: 4312-4990

Zapatos rojos (San Telmo)
(milonga, shows)
Balcarce 460.
Tel.: 4372-6179

Club Gricel (San Cristobal)
La Rioja 1180
Tel.: 4857-7157

Souvenirs de tango
Tango souvenirs
(posters/ afiches)

Club del Tango (San Nicolás)
Paraná 123 5° of. 114
Tel.: 4372-7251

Galería Solar de French (San Telmo)

María de San Telmo
Pasaje de la Defensa (San Telmo)

El quiosco del Tango (San Nicolás)
Corrientes 1512 esq. Paraná

Centro de Exposiciones Caminito
(La Boca)
Lamadrid 784/90 esq. Caminito

Galería Caminito (La Boca)
Del Valle Iberlucea 1151
Tel.: 4301-1520

Chamote (San Telmo)
Defensa 861

Láminas antiguas (San Telmo)
Defensa 832

Buenos Aires Souvenirs (San Telmo)
Defensa 1066 local 10

Caminito Tango (La Boca)
Magallanes 827

Pasaje Obelisco Norte (San Nicolás)
Ella y yo, Local 5 y 7

Almacén de Tangos Generales
(San Telmo)
Plaza Dorrego

Tradiciones Argentinas
Ayacucho 1958 y Posadas 1167

Instituciones de tango

Academia Porteña del Lunfardo
Estados Unidos 1379
Tel.: 4383-2393

Academia Nacional del Tango
Av. de Mayo 833 1° piso
Tel.: 4345-6967

Casa Museo de Carlos Gardel
Jean Jaures 763

Tumba de Carlos Gardel
Av. Guzmán 780 (Chacarita)

Argentine Folklore

Rhythms and dances

Apart from the Tango, the Plata River folklore, you may find dances and music in Buenos Aires from every region of Argentina. Many are the rhythms. On the coast, the chamamé stands out, in the pampas, the zamba, towards the north, the chacarera, and at the border with Bolivia, the carnavalito. There are over hundred dances and native songs. Here, we only show a few that we consider to be representative.

Carnavalito.

Pericón.

Zamba.

Malambo.

Chamamé.

Bailecito.

Gato.

Instruments and folk attires.

Modern Creole Garments.

Creole guitar.

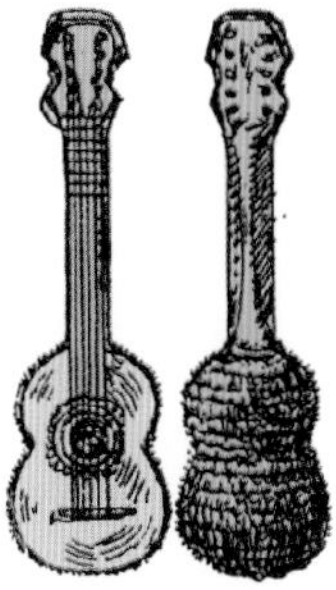

Tubular Bass drum.

Quena.

Modern attires from the North.

"Charango" Front and back.

Siku.

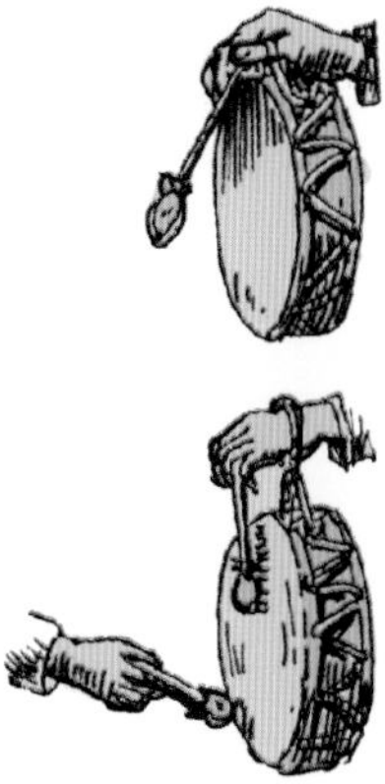

Old Creole attire.

Box, two ways of playing

Flat Bass Drum.

Bovine races and their cuts

Las Argentine meat is famous everywhere because of its outstanding quality. The natural breeding of livestock in the wide pastures of the pampas combined with a mild weather result in a meat, that makes it impossible for someone not to try an Asado Criollo (Creole Barbecue). For this purpose, there are a lot of good restaurants, grill rooms, and BBQ restaurants (see p. 155).

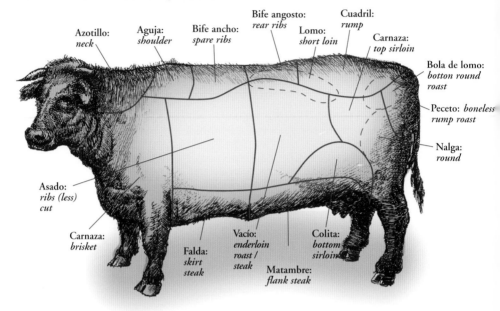

Azotillo: *neck*
Aguja: *shoulder*
Bife ancho: *spare ribs*
Bife angosto: *rear ribs*
Lomo: *short loin*
Cuadril: *rump*
Carnaza: *top sirloin*
Bola de lomo: *botton round roast*
Peceto: *boneless rump roast*
Nalga: *round*
Asado: *ribs (less) cut*
Carnaza: *brisket*
Falda: *skirt steak*
Vacío: *enderloin roast / steak*
Matambre: *flank steak*
Colita: *bottom sirloin*

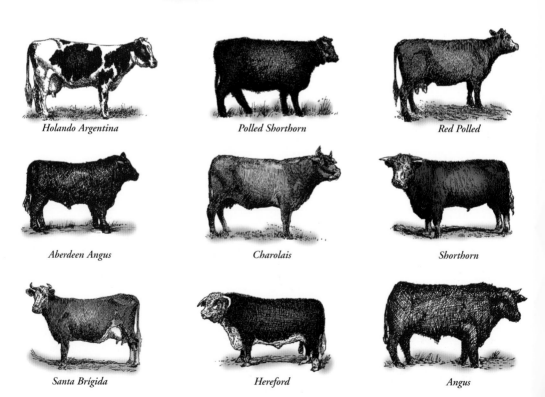

Holando Argentina

Polled Shorthorn

Red Polled

Aberdeen Angus

Charolais

Shorthorn

Santa Brígida

Hereford

Angus

Meat cut

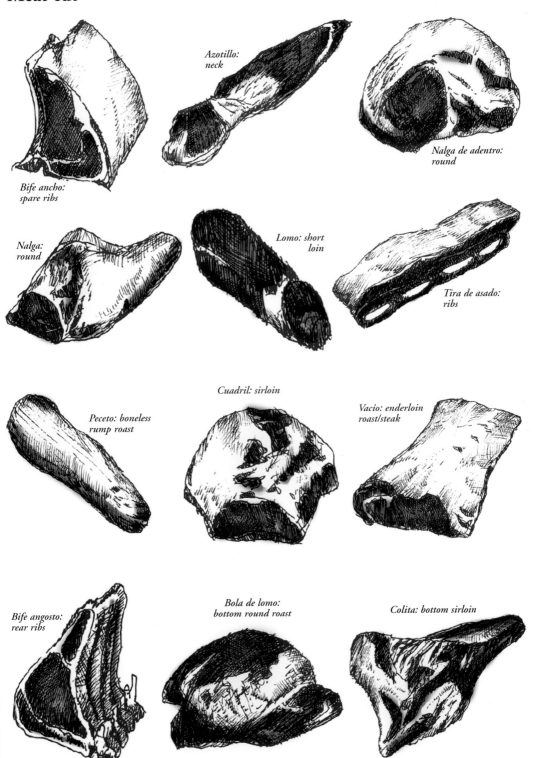

Bife ancho:
spare ribs

Azotillo:
neck

Nalga de adentro:
round

Nalga:
round

Lomo: short
loin

Tira de asado:
ribs

Peceto: boneless
rump roast

Cuadril: sirloin

Vacío: enderloin
roast/steak

Bife angosto:
rear ribs

Bola de lomo:
bottom round roast

Colita: bottom sirloin

The argentine asado

Vertical or cross rosting pit

Costillar:
ribs

Lechón:
sucling pig

Wood fire. You
light it with
little branches
and soft wood
inside the pile.

Coal fire. You
light the fire
with paper
and little
branches.

Chivito:
Goat

Horizontal roasting grill

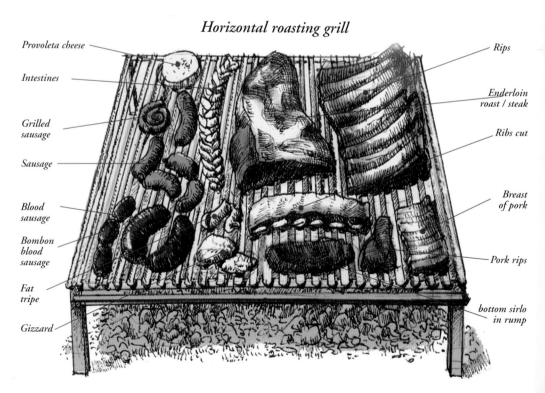

Provoleta cheese

Intestines

Grilled
sausage

Sausage

Blood
sausage

Bombon
blood
sausage

Fat
tripe

Gizzard

Rips

Enderloin
roast / steak

Ribs cut

Breast
of pork

Pork rips

bottom sirlo
in rump

El gaucho

Garments and mount
El apero

Sudadera.

Full length apron.

Carona of leather.

Cinch.

Hijar.

Lomillo.

Cojinillo.

Although the archetypical character of the city is the tanguero, milonguero, or compadrito; in neighborhoods like Mataderos or in many folk parties (see page 134) you are bound to make contact with the archetypical character of the pampas: the Gaucho, with his original attire and all the equestrian culture he develops.

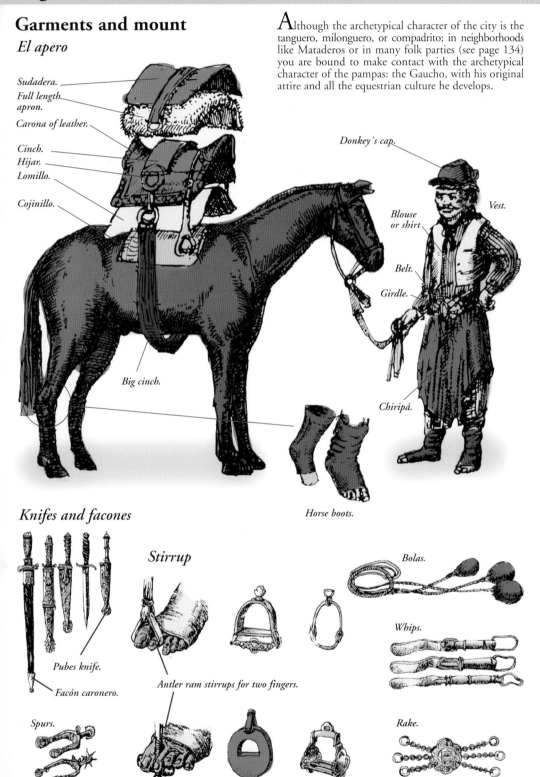

Donkey's cap.

Vest.

Blouse or shirt.

Belt.

Girdle.

Big cinch.

Chiripá.

Horse boots.

Knifes and facones

Pubes knife.

Facón caronero.

Stirrup

Antler ram stirrups for two fingers.

Bolas.

Whips.

Spurs.

Rake.

Mate

What we call mate is an infusion with a nice taste and drinking it with friends has become such a widespread tradition that we might say it is a national custom. The Guaraní tribes discovered the plant it is made up of, which is called yerba, and they also found that its leaves are good for people's health.

The Jesuits later started to drink it as tea (in mate bags) and they created a system for growing the herb or plant (yerba paraguensi) that we use to make mate.

The way we make and drink this infusion is also taken from the Guaraní tribes, which proves how ingenious their culture used to be. The gourd (also called mate), the straw (which we use to zip the drink), the kettle and the yerba are the basic elements you need if you want to drink some good mate.

Mate as a word has two different meanings: on the one hand, it is the drink itself and, on the other hand, it is the gourd, which also has different names

according to the size, namely: the big ones are called porongos and those that have flat sides are called galletas.

Even though all mates were made out of pumpkins at the beginning, nowadays almost any material is good enough to pour some yerba and water in it. Some of them have silver decorations and others are entirely made up of silver or China.

The straw or bombilla is the means by which we zip the liquid. It has been a metal straw since the Jesuits' times, but the Guaraní tribes used to have cane straws.

Sharing your mate and bombilla is a token of good manners, fraternity and peace.

Mate as a drink may take several names according to the way you make it, namely:

Bitter mate or cimarrón: just plain hot water and yerba.

Sweet mate: hot water, yerba, and sugar (white or brown).

Tereré: cold mate. You may use either cold water or citric fruits' juice.

Milk mate: hot milk and yerba.

Mate with coffee: yerba and hot coffee.

Mate Cocido: served as tea either in teabags or boiling the yerba. You may add some milk.

Gastronomic guide

LA BOCA

Caminito Tango Show
Del Valle Iberlucea 1151
Te. 4301-1520/30
Cocina internacional /
International cuisine

Campo e Mare
Lamadrid 701 Tel. 4302-0785
Parrilla / Argentine barbecue

Cantina Gennarino
Necochea 1210 Tel. 4301-6617
Cocina italiana / Seafood

El Obrero
Cafarena 64 Tel. 4362-9912
Cocina argentina / Argentine cuisine

El Puentecito
Luján 2101 Tel. 4301-1794
Parrila / Argentine cuisine

La Barbería
Av. Pedro de Mendoza 19598
Tel. 4301-8870
Pescados y mariscos / Seafood

Il Matterello
Martín Rodríguez 517 Tel. 4307-0529
Cocina italiana / Italian cuisine

Il Piccolo Vapore
Necochea 1190 Tel. 4301-4455
Cocina italiana / Italian Cuisine

La Ribera
Av. Pedro de Mendoza 1875
Tel. 4301-5160

La Cancha
Brandsen 697 Tel. 4362-2975
Pescados y mariscos / Seafood

Valle de Palos
Aristóbulo del Valle 600
Tel. 4300-0671
Cocina casera / Home made cuisine

Viejo Puente de Mario
Av. Alte. Brown 1499 Tel. 4301-2170
Pescados y mariscos / Seafodd

SAN TELMO • MONTSERRAT.

Asociación Sueca
Tacuarí 147 Tel. 4334-7813/9552
Cocina sueca / Swedish Cuisine

Ban/Juu
México 1424 Tel. 4381-1259
Cocina japonesa / Japanese cusine

Bidou de las Luces
Perú 269 Tel. 4801- 1844
Cocina argentina / Argentine cuisine

Basque Francés
Moreno 1370
Tel. 4382-0244 / 383-5021
Cocina vasco francés/ Basque cuisine

Campo dei Fiori
San José 491 Tel. 4381-1800/8402
Cocina italiana / Italian cuisine

Centro Asturiano
Solís 475 Tel. 4381-1342
Cocina española / Spanish cuisine

Club español
Bernardo de Irigoyen 180
Tel.:4342-4380

Vasco Fermín
Moreno 1370

Laurak Bat (Cocina vasca)
Av. Belgrano 1144
Tel.: 4381-0682

Como en casa
H. Yrigoyen 1315 Tel. 4383-2865
Cocina argentina / Argentine cuisine

El acuerdo
Moreno 360 Tel. 4331-4172

El Caserío
H. Irigoyen 575 tel. 4331-1336

El Globo
H. Yrigoyen 1199 Tel. 381-3926
Cocina española / Spanish cuisine

El Querandí
Perú 302 Tel. 4345-0331/ 1770
Cocina argentina / Argentine cuisine

El Rocío
Salta 151 tel. 4381-7502
Cocina internacional /
International cuisine

La María
México 1310 tel. 4383-0173
Pastas

La Posada de Don Quijote
Lima 387 Tel. 4383-8602
Cocina internacional /
International cuisine

La Tasca
H. Yrigoyen 1218 tel. 4381-1290

Mesón Español
H. Yrigoyen 1211 1° tel. 4384-6667
Cocina española / Spanish cuisine

Morocco
H. Yrigoyen 851 Tel. 4342-6046
Cocina exótica / Exotic cuisine

New Shushina
Solís 275 Tel. 4372-1056
Cocina japonesa / Japanese cuisine

Plaza Mayor
Venezuela 1399 tel. 4383-0788
Cocina española /
Spanish cuisine

Prosciutto
Venezuela 1212
Tel. 4383-8058
Cocina italiana / italian cuisine

Rivero al Sur
Luis Saenz peña Esq. Estados Unidos
Cena show / Dinner show

Status Virrey Ceballos 178
Tel. 4372- 6282 / 382-8531

Vieja Victoria
H. Yrigoyen 778
Tel. 4372-6282 /4316
Parrila / Argentine barbecue

PALERMO • LAS CAÑITAS

El Mistyco
(Cocina Porteña)
Gorriti 5902
Tel.: 4775-3653

Tango Republic (Mediterranea)
Julian Alvarez 1998
Tel.: 4864-4507

El Federal (Cocina criolla)
Honduras 5254
Tel.: 4382-6500

Almacén Cabrera
Cabrera 4399 Tel. 4832-4670
Cocina criolla / Native cuisine

Al Shark
Av. Scalabrini Ortiz 1550
Tel. 4833-2049/6933
Cocina arabe / Arabian cuisine

Azafrán
Honduras 5143 Tel. 4832-6487
Cocina casera / Home made cuisine

Bella Italia
Rep. Arabe Siria 3285
Tel. 4802-4253
Cocina italiana / Italian cuisine

Buenos Aires News
Paseo de la Infanta
Av. del Libertador y
Av. de la Infanta
Tel. 4778-1500 / 0127
Cocina Internacional /
internationale cuisine

Cala
Soler 4065 Tel.4823-0413
Cocina francesa / french cuisine

Campo Alto
Arenales 3360 Tel. 4821-6030 /6059
Cocina argentina / Argentine cuisine

Cangas de Narcea
Av. Godoy Cruz 3108
Tel. 4773-4601 / 6706
Cocina internacional /
International cuisine

Casona María María
Güemez 3140 Tel. 4821-3817
Cocina italiana / Italian cuisine

Centro de la Olla
Jorge Luis Borges 1559
Pizza y pasta

Cielito Lindo
El Salvador 4999 Tel. 4832-8054
Cocina mexicana / mexican cuisine

Club del Golf
Av. Tornquist 6385
Tel. 4775-0148 / 0197
Cocina internacional / International cuisine

Cosa Nostra
Cabrera 4270 tel. 4862-1906
Cocina italiana / italian cuisine

Cristophe
Fitz Roy 1994 Tel. 4771-1155
Cocina francesa / French cuisine

Del Tomate
Salguero 2963 Tel. 4804-7882
Pastas

Dimitri. Puente Mitre
Av. Caseros y vías del ferrocarril
Tel. 4806-0022
Cena show / dinner show

Dolli .Av. Figueroa Alcorta 3004
Tel. 4806-3366 / 3257
Cocina internacional /
International cuisine

Domani
Salguero 3000 Tel. 4807-5288
Pizza y pasta

Don Battaglia
Av. Scalabrini Ortiz 803
Tel. 4773-0484 / 0597
Cocina Argentina / Argentine cuisine

Doney
Av. Del Libertador 3096
Tel. 4802-0075
Minutas / Fast Food

El Beduino
Av. Scalabrini Ortiz 1453
Tel. 4831-6951
Cocina internacional /
International cuisine

El Lugar de Angel
Av. Del Libertador 4534
Tel. 4771-3179
Cocina internacional /
Internatiional cuisine

El Oso del Charlie
Av. Del Libertador 4534
Tel. 4771-9184
Cocina internacional /
International cuisine

El Sheik
Rep. Arabe Siria 3330
Tel. 4806-1398
Cocina arabe / Arabian cuisine

El Taller
Honduras 4988 Tel. 4831-5501
Minutas / Fast food

Beckett bar, restaurant,
galeria de arte.
El Salvador 4960. Tel. 4831-7373

El Trapiche
Paraguay 5099 Tel. 4772-7343
Cocina internacional /
International cuisine

Gascón
Av. Córdoba y Gascón
Tel. 4862-9662
Cocina internacional /
International cuisine

Gitana Bs. As. News
Paseo de la Infanta
Av. del Libertador Tel. 4778-1500
Cocina española / Spanish cuisine

Guido's
Rep. de la India 2843
Tel. 4802-2391
Pastas

Gastronomic guide

Habano
Seguí 4674 Tel. 4777-1043
Cocina Internacional /
International cuisine

Hermann
Av. Santa Fe 3902
Tel. 4382-1929
Cocina Alemana /
German cuisine

Incontro
Guatemala 5602 tel. 4775-7016
Cocina Italiana / Italian cuisine

Lusef
Malabia 1378 Tel. 4773-0450
Cocina Siria / Ssyrian cuisine

Jade
Ugarteche 3033 tel. 4803-2838
Cocina china / Chinese cuisine

Kalaat Yandal
Malabia 1467
Tel. 4831-1587
Cocina Arabe / Arabian cuisine

Katmandú
Av. Córdoba 3447
Tel. 4963-1122 / 3250
Cocina Huindú / Hindu cuisine

Kisher's
Av Cordoba 4660 tel. 4773-1888
Cocina Judía / Jewish cuisine

La Boguedita
Gascón 1460 Tel. 4867-1619
Cocina Cubana / Cuban cuisine

La Canzonetta
Av. Dorrego 1556 Tel. 4771-3998
Cocina Italiana / Italian cuisine

La Capillita
Av. Dorrego 2898 Tel. 4778-0068
Pescados y Mariscos / Seafood

La Casa Polaca
Jorge Luis Borges 2076
Tel. 4774-7621
Cocina Polaca / Polish cuisine

La Copa de Oro de Carlitos
Olleros 1667 Tel. 4772-5244
Parrilla / Argentine barbecue

La Furchina
Paraguay 3839 tel. 4776-2835
Cocina Italiana / Italian cuisine

La Mamá Rosa
Jufré 202 tel. 4773-2913
Cocina Argentina / Argentine cuisine

La Placita
Jorge Luis Borges 1636
Tel. 4832-6444
Cocina Italiana / Italian cuisine

Las Violetas
Av. Scalabrini Ortiz 2680
Tel. 4832-3968 / 1392
Parrilla / Argentine barbecue

La Tranquera
Av. Figueroa Alcorta 6464
Tel. 4784-6119
Parrilla / Argentine barbecue

Lindo Jardín
Cabello 3419 Tel. 4802-6851
Cocina China / Chinese cuisine

Morizono
Paraguay 3521 Tel. 4823-4250
Cocina Japonesa / Japanese cuisine

Museo Renault
Av. Figueroa Alcorta 3301
Tel. 4802-9629
Cocina Japonesa / Japanese cuisine

Nacachi
Jorge Luis Borges 1627
Tel. 4833-3311
Minutas / Fast food

Octavio
Salguero 2743 Tel. 4806-0035
Pastas

Oviedo
Beruti 2602
Tel. 4822-5415 / 4821- 3711
Cocina Española / Spanish cuisine

Paper Moon
Cerviño 3732
Tel. 4805-4643
Cocina Francesa / french cuisine

Park Zoo
Av. Sarmiento 2725
Tel. 4806-1835
Internacional cocina / International cuisine

Pimienta
Paraguay 3512
Tel. 4824-7590
Cocina Argentina / Argentine cuisine

Pizza Cero
Cerviño 3701 Tel. 4803-3449
Pizzas

Pizza Donna
Av. Santa Fe 3202 Tel. 4822-4206
Pizzas

Plaka
Arévalo 2725 Tel. 4777-6051
Cocina Griega / Grek cuisine

Puerto Sol
Bulnes 2593 Tel. 4802-8640
Cocina Argentina / Argentine cuisine

Provoletto
Huergo 190 tel. 4778- 3001
Parrilla / Argentine barbecue

Rincón Orgánico
Gurruchaga y Castillo
Tel. 4777-5082
Cocina Australiana

Rock Garden (Cocina Internacional)
Ugarteche 3154 tel. 4806-9178

Romario (Pizzas)
Cabello 3700 Tel. 4802-4732

Sahara
Cabrera 4223
Cocina Arabe / Arabian cuisine

Salguero y el Río
Av. Rafael Obligado y Salguero
Tel. 4801-5422 Minutas / Fast Food

Sarkis
Thames 1101
Tel. 4772-4911
Cocina Arabe / Arabian cuisine

Scuzi I
Cabello 3601 Tel. 4804-2900
Cocina Internacional /
International cuisine

Sítara
La Pampa 735 tel. 4784-2160
Cocina Hindú-Pakistaní /
Hindu-Pakistanese cuisine
Súbito
Salguero 2741 tel. 4806-0033
Pizza y Pasta

Tabaré
Charcas 3387 Telefax 4821-7598
Parrilla / Argentine barbecue

Tago Mago
Av. Rafael Obligado y Salguero
Tel. 4804-2444
Cocina Argentina / Argentine cuisine

Te Mataré Ramirez
Paraguay 4062
Tel. 4831-9156
Cocina Exótica / Exotic cuisine

The Horse
Av. Del Libertador 3880
Tel. 4773-4847
Cocina Internacional /
International cuisine

Xalapa
El Salvador 4800 Tel. 4833-6102
Cocina Mexicana / Mexican cuisine

Yamani
Julián Alvarez 1939 Tel. 4862-2848
Cocina vegetariana /
Vegetarian cuisine

Yasmin
Cabrera 4625 tel. 4832-5278
Cocina Libanesa / Lebanese cuisine

PUERTO MADERO
Agua Dulce
Av. Ing. Huergo 400 Tel. 4345-0900
Cocina internacional /
International cuisine

Bahía Madero (Pizzas)
Av. A. Moreau de Justo 292
Tel. 4319-8733

Bice
Av. A Moreau de Justo 192
Tel. 4315-6216
Cocina Italiana / Italian Cuisine

Divino Buenos Aires
Cecilia Grierson 28
tel. 4312-1221
Cocina internacional

Dizzy Lizzy
Av. A Moreau de Justo 846
Cocina Estadounidense /
American cuisine

Dock Café
Av. A Moreau de Justo 350/40
Tel. 4319-8719
Minutas / Fast Food

El Mirasol del Puerto
Av. A Moreau de Justo 202
Tel. 4315-6277
Cocina Argentina

Fechoría
Av. A Moreau de Justo 1140
Tel. 4342-8609/4949
Cocina Italiana / Italian cuisine

Hereford (Parrilla)
Av. A Moreau de Justo 1140
Tel. 4319-8715

Il Gatto Trattorías
Av. A Moreau de Justo 1192
Tel. 4345-6565/4949
Cocina Italiana / Italian cuisine

La Caballeriaza
Av. A Moreau de Justo 580
Tel. 4314-2648/50

La Casona de Roque
Av. A Moreau de Justo 256
Tel. 4315-6343
Cocine Italiana / Italian cuisine

La Parolaccia
Av. A Moreau de Justo 1052
Tel. 4343-1679/4742/1345
Cocina italiana / Italian cuisine

La Rosada
Av. A Moreau de Justo 1170
Tel. 4313-7200
Cocina Internacional /
International cuisine

Liberpool Pub
Av. A Moreau de Justo 350
Tel. 4319-8723
Minutas / Fast food

Piperno
Av. A Moreau de Justo 1942
Tel. 4313-0600

Puerto Cristal
Av. A Moreau de Justo 1080
Tel. 4331-3309/3669
Pizza y Pasta

Puerto Sorrento
Av. A Moreau de Justo 410
Tel. 4319-8730
Cocina Internacional /
International cuisine

Rodizio
Av. A Moreau de Justo 840
Tel. 4334-3646/3638
Cocina Internacional /
International cuisine

Spell Café
Av. A Moreau de Justo 740
Tel. 4334-0512
Cocina Internacional /
International cuisine

Spettus Steak House
Av. A Moreau de Justo 876
Tel. 4334-4210/4126
Cocina Brasilera /
Brazilian cuisine

Tocorro (Cocina Cubana)
Av. A Moreau de Justo 1050
Tel. 4342-6032

Gastronomic guide

Xcaret
Av. A Moreau de Justo 164
Tel. 4315-6260/61
Cocina Internacional /
International cuisine

RECOLETA

A la Maracosa
M.T. de Alvear 225
Cocina Italiana / Italian cuisine

A'Mamma Liberata
J.E.Uriburu 1755
Tel.4804-3638
Cocina Italiana / Italian cuisine

Armenoville
Av. Alvear 1879
Tel. 4804-1033
Cena Show / Dinner Show

Au Bec Fin
Vicente López 1827
Tel. 44801-6894
Cocina Francesa / French cuisine

Babieca
Av. Santa Fe 1898 Tel. 4813-4914
Pizzas

Bonifacio
Guido 1939 Tel. 4805-2336 / 3996
Cocina Arabe / Arabian cuisine

Burger King
Av. Santa Fe 1997 Tel. 4812-5891
Fast Food

Campos del Pilar.
Buenos Aires Design
Av. Pueyrredón 2501
Tel. 4806-1111 int. 1276
Parrilla / Argentine barbecue

Caruso. Buenos Aires Design
Av. Pueyrredón 2501
Tel. 4806-3299
Cocina Italiana / Italian cuisine

Champs Ellysees.
Buenos Aires Design
Av. Pueyrredón 2501 Tel. 4806-1111
Minutas / Fast food

Clark's Recoleta
Junín 1777 Tel. 4801-9502
Cocina Internacional /
International cuisine

Como
Juncal 2019 Tel. 4806-9664 / 7954
Cocina Internacional /
International cuisine

El Beso
Pacheco de Melo 2909
Cocina Exótica / Exotic cuisine

El Bodegón de Peña
Peña 2475 Tel. 4806-7536
Cocina Argentina /
Argentine cuisine

El Living
M. T. de Alvear 1540
Tel. 4811-4730

El Tranvía
Av. Santa Fe 2933 Tel. 4823-6347
Pizza y Pasta

Fellini
Paraná 1209 Tel. 4811-2222
Cocina Italiana / Italian cuisine

Hard Rock Café.
Buenos Aires Design
Av. Pueyrredón 2501
Tel. 4807-7625
Cocina Estadounidense /
American cuisine

Harper's Junín
Junín 1773 Tel. 4801-7140
Cocina Internacional /
International cuisine

Hippopotamus
Junín 1787 Tel. 4801-1040
Cocina Internacional /
International cuisine

La Barra
Av. Del Libertador 932
Tel. 4812-1745
Cocina Española /
Spanish cuisine

La Biela
Av. Quintana 596
Tel. 4804-0449
Minutas / Fast food

La Mansión. Park Hyatt Hotel
Cerrito 1455 Tel. 4326-3610
Cocina Francesa / French cuisine

La Parolaccia
Riobamba 1046 Tel. 4812-1053
Cocina Italiana / Italian cuisine

Lola
R. M. Ortíz 1805 tel. 4804-3410
Cocina Internacional /
International cuisine

Luckie's. Buenos Aires Desin
Av. Pueyrredón 2501 Tel. 4806-1111
Cocina Estadounidense /
American cuisine

Mc Donald's
Av. Córdoba 2031 Tel. 4964-0625
Fast Food

Mora X
Vicente López 2152
Tel. 4803-0261 / 2646
Cocina Francesa / french cuisine

Munich del Pilar.
Buenos Aires Design
Av. Pueyrredón 2501
Tel. 4806-1111 / 6910

Open Plaza
Av. Del Libertador 1800
Tel. 4802-7501 / 03
Fast food

Pizza Banana
Ayacucho 1425 Tel. 4812-6321
Pizza y Pasta

Porto Bello
J. E. Uriburu 1629 Tel. 4806-4275

Rodizio
Av. Callao 1292 Tel. 4814-1776
Cocina Internacional /
International cuisine

Romanaccio
Av. Callao 1021 Tel. 4811-9888
Pizza y Pasta

Sahara Continental
Junín 1733 Tel. 4801-7544
Cocina Internacional /
International cuisine

Sensu
Posadas 1101 Tel. 4815-5161
Cocina Japonesa / Japanese cuisine

Teatriz
Riobamba 1220 Tel. 4811-1915
Cocina Internacional /
International cuisine

The Kilkenny. Irish Pub
M. T. De Alvear 399 Tel. 4312-7291
Restaurante Irlandés y Continental

The Shamrock
Rodríguez Peña 1220 Tel. 4812-3584
Cocina Irlandesa / Irish cuisine

Tiro Loco
Vicente López y Azcuénaga
Cocina Mexicana / Mexican cuisine

Troyka
Juncal 1647 Tel. 4414-1009
Cocina Rusa / Russian cuisine

RETIRO • PLAZA SAN MARTIN

A Mi Manera
Av. Del Libertador 308
Cocina Italiana / Italian cuisine

Blue Oyster
M. T. De Alvear 399
Tel. 4312-9179
Pescados y Mariscos

Club del Retiro
Juncal 743 Tel. 4326-7869
Parrilla / Argentine Barbecue

Dixie Diner
Av. Del Libertador y C. Pellegrini
Tel. 4322-3646
Cocina Estadounidense /
American cuisine

Don Corleone Blues Bar
Reconquista 924 Tel. 4311-8802
Cocina Italiana / Italian cuisine

Druid Inn
Reconquista 1040
Tel. 4312-9844
Cocina Internacional /
International cuisine

El Aljibe- Sheraton Hotel
San Martín 1225
Tel. 4318-9000
Cocina Internacional /
International cuisine

Filo (Pizzas)
San Martín 975
Tel. 4311-0312 / 1871

Frontera
Esmeralda 941
Tel. 4313-0013
Cocina Internacional /
International cuisine

Galani. Marriot Plaza Hotel
Posadas 1086 Tel. 4326-1234
Cocina Italiana / Italian cuisine

Jan Toki
Posadas 1029 Tel. 4393-0332
Cocina Vasca / Basque cuicine

La Brasseire. Marriot Plaza Hotel
Florida 1005 Tel. 4318-3000
Cocina Internacional /
International cuisine

La Chacra
Av. Córdoba 941
Tel. 4322-1419 / 2593
Parrilla / Argentine barbecue

La Payanca
Suipacha 1015 Tel. 4312-5209
Cocina Criolla / Native cuisine

La Querencia
Esmeralda 1392
Tel. 4393-3205 / 3202
Cocina Criolla / Native cuisine

La Terraza Anush.
Lancaster Hotel
Av. Córdoba 405 Tel. 4311-3021
Cocina Argentina-Arabe /
Argentine-Arabian cuisine

Las Nazarenas
Reconquista 1132 Tel. 4312-5559
Cocina Argentina /
Argentine cuisine

Ligure
Juncal 855 Tel. 4393-0644
Cocina Internacional /
International cuisine

Morizono
Paraguay y Reconquista
Tel. 4314-0924 / 4443
Cocina Japonesa / Japanese cuisine

Orleans.
Aspen Towers Hotel
Paraguay 857
Tel. 4312-9172

Piola
Libertad 1078
Tel. 4812-0690
Cocina Italiana / Italian cuisine

Plaza Mayor
Posadas 1052 Tel. 4393-5671
Cocina Española /
Spanish cuisine

Romario
Montevideo 1655
Tel. 4814-5210
Pizzas

Sensu
San Martín 760
Tel. 4319-5103
Cocina Japonesa
Japanese cuisine

The Tower Lounge.
Sheraton Hotel
Av. Leandro N. Alem 1193
Tel. 4318-9000 int. 2510
Cocina Internacional /
International cuisine

Tridimensional guide of Buenos Aires

MUSEUMS

Museo de Arte Moderno
Museum of Modern Arts
Av. San Juan 350
Tel.: 4361-1121

Museo Histórico Nacional
National Historic Museum
Defensa 1600
Tel.: 4307-1182

Museo Penitenciario "Antonio Ballve"
Penitenciary Museum
"Antonio Ballve"
Humberto 1° 378
Tel.: 4362-0099

Museo de Arte Hispanoamericano
"Isaac Fernández Blanco"
Museum of Spanish-American Art
"Isaac Fernández Blanco"
Suipacha 1422
Tel.: 4327-0228/0272

Museo Participativo de Ciencias
Participative Museum of Science
Junín 1930
Tel.: 4807-3260/4806-3456

Museo Nacional de Bellas Artes
National Fine Arts Museum
Av. Del Libertador 1473
Tel.: 4803-0802/8814

Museo Nacional de Arte Decorativo
National Decorative Arts Museum
Av. Del Libertador 1902
Tel.: 4806-8306/4801-8248

Museo de Arte Oriental
Oriental Arts Museum
Av. Del Libertador 1902 Piso 1°
Tel.: 4801-5988

Museo de Motivos Argentinos
"José Hernández"
Museum of Argentine Heritage
"José Hernández"
Av. Del Libertador 2373
Tel.: 4802-7294/4803-2384

MALBA, Museo de Arte
Latinoamericano de Buenos Aires.
Av. Figueroa Alcorta 3415 (Palermo)
Tel.: 4808-6500

Museo de Artes Plásticas
"Eduardo Sívori"
Museum of Plastic Arts
"Eduardo Sívori"
Av. De la Infanta Isabel 555
Tel.: 4774-9452

Museo Casa de Yrurtia
Yrurtia´s House Museum
O´ Higgins 2390
Tel.: 4781-0385

Museo de Arte Español
"Enrique Larreta"
Spanish Art Museum
"Enrique Larreta"
Juramento 2291
Tel.: 4783-2640/4748-4040

Museo Histórico Sarmiento
Sarmiento Historic Museum
Juramento 2180
Tel.: 4783-7555

Museo Histórico de la Ciudad
de Bs. As. "Brigadier Gral.
Cornelio de Saavedra"
Crisólogo Larralde 6309
Tel.: 4572-0746

Museo de Ciencias Naturales
"Bernardino Rivadavia"
Museum of Natural Science
Angel Gallardo 470
Tel.: 4982-1154

Museo Xul Solar. Laprida 1212
Tel.: 4824-3302

ART GALLERIES

Del Infinito: Av. Quintana 325
Dabbah Torrejon: Bustamante 1187
Principium: Esmeralda 1357
Gara: Pje. Soria 5020
Belleza y felicidad: A.de Figueroa 900
Elsi del Río: Arevalo 1748
Braga Menendez Schuster: Darwin 1154
Atica: Libertad 1240
MAMAN Av. del Libertador 2475
De Santi: M.T.de Alvear 868
El Socorro: Suipacha 1331
Gal.Museo Aguilar: Suipacha 1178
Klemm: M.T. de Alvear 636
Lagard: Suipacha 1216
Le Point: Suipacha 1250
Leonardo Avalos: Arroyo 858
Palatina: Arroyo 821
Praxis Arte Internacional:
Arenales 1311
Rubbers: Suipacha 1175
Ruth Benzacar: Florida 1000
Artistas Plásticos: Viamonte 458
Suipacha: Suipacha 1248
Van Eyck: Sta.Fe 834
Van Riel: Talcahuano 1257
Vermeer Galería de Arte:
Suipacha 1168
VyP: Arroyo 971
Zurbarán: Cerrito 1522
Espacio Giesso: Defensa 1326
Sara García Uriburu: Uruguay 1223
Art House: Uruguay 1223

CINEMAS

Alto Palermo: Av. Santa Fe 3235 -
827-8362
Ambasador: Lavalle 777 - 322-9700
América: Callao 1057 - 811-3818
Atlas Belgrano: Av. Cabildo 2165 -
781-7200
Atlas Lavalle: Lavalle 869 - 322-1936
Atlas Recoleta: Guido 1952 -
803-3313
Atlas Santa Fe: Av. Santa Fe 2015 -
823-7878
Auditorio Maxi: Carlos Pellegrini
657 - 326-1822
Belgrano Multiplex: Obligado y
Mendoza: 781-8183
Capitol: Av. Santa Fe 1848 -
812-2379
Cineplex: Lavalle 727 - 393-8610
Complejo Tita Merello: Suipacha
442 - 322-1195
Electric Lavalle: Lavalle 836 -
322-1846
Galerías Pacífico: Florida 735 - 319-
5357
Gamount: Rivadavia 1635 - 371-
3050
General Paz: Av. Cabildo 2702 -
781-1412
Grand Splendid: Av. Santa Fe 1860 -

812-0808
Leopoldo Lugones: Av. Corrientes
1530 - 374-8611
Lorange: Av. Corrientes 1372 -
373-2411
Lorca: Av. Corrientes 1428 -
371-5017
Los Angeles: Av. Corrients 177/70 -
371-3742
Losuar: Av. Corrientes 1743 -
4371-6100
Maxi 1-2-3: C.Pellegrini 657 -
4326-1822
Metro: Cerrito 570 - 4382-4219
Monumental: Lavalle 780 -
4393-8865
Normandie: Lavalle 855 -
4322-1000
Ocean: Lavalle 739 - 4322-1515
Paseo Alcorta: Av. F. Alcorta y
Salguero: 4806-5665
Patio Bullrich: Av. Libertador 750 -
4815-8328
Premier: Av. Corrientes 1565 -
4374-2113
Santa Fe: Av. Santa Fe 1947 -
4812-8980
Savoy: Av. Cabildo 2829 -
4781-9400
Solar de la Abadía: Luis M. Campos
y Maure - 778-5181
Trocadero: Lavalle 820 - 4393-8321.

THEATERS

Astral: Av. Corrientes 1639 -
4374-5707
Ateneo: Paraguay 918 - 4328-2888
Avenida: Av. de Mayo 1222 -
4381-0662
Blanca Podestá: Av. Corrientes 1283
4382-2592
Broadway: Av. Corrientes 1155 -
4382-2345
Cátulo Castillo: Bmé. Mitre 970 -
4345-2774
Cervantes: Libertad 815 - 816-4224
Colón: Libertad 621 - 382-5414
Del Centro: Sarmiento 1249 -
417-7097
Del Globo: M.T. de Alvear 1155 -
4816-3307
Del Pueblo: Diag. Norte 943 -
4326-3606
Del Sur: Venezuela 1286 -
4383-5702
El Excéntrico: Lerma 47
Empire: H.l Yrigoyen 1934 -
4953-8254
General San Martín: Av. Corrientes
1530 - 4371-0118
Gran Rex: Corrientes 900 -
4322-8000
La Plaza: Av. Corrientes 1660 -
4371-7623
La Trastienda: Balcarce 460 -
4342-7650
Liberarte: Av. Corrientes 1555 -
4375-2341
Liceo: Rivadavia y Paraná -
4381-4291
Lola Membrives: Av. Corrientes
1280 - 383-2025
Maipo: Esmeralda 433 - 322-4882
Manzana de las Luces: Perú 294 -
342-9930
Margarita Xirgu : Chacabuco 875 -
300-2448
Metropolitan: Av. Corrientes 1343 -
371-0816

Off Corrientes: Av. Corrientes 1632
- 4373-3608
Opera: Corrientes 900 - 4326-1335
Payró: San Martín 766 - 4312-5922
Picadilly Teatro: Av. Corrientes 1254
- 4373-1900
Piccolo Teatro: Av. Corrientes 1624 -
4373-3465
Presidente Alvear: Av. Corrientes
1659 - 374-6076
Megafón: Chacabuco 1072.

SHOPPINGS / MALLS

Abasto
Av. Corrientes 3247
Tel.: 4959-3400

Alto Avellaneda
Guemes 897
Avellaneda

Alto Palermo
Arenales 3360
Tel.: 4821-6030/6059

Buenos Aires Design Recoleta
Av. Pueyrredón 2501

Caballito Shopping Center
Av. Rivadavia 5108

Galerías Pacífico
Florida y Av. Córdoba

Paseo Alcorta
Jerónimo Salguero 3172

Easy Home Center
Av. Bullrich 345 y Cerviño
Paseo La Plaza
Av. Corrientes 1660

Patio Bullrich
Av. Del Libertador 750 y
Posadas 1245

Solar de la Abadía
Luis María Campos y Maure

Spinetto Shopping Center
Moreno 2301
Tel.: 4954-3252 al 59

SIGHTS

Jardín Zoológico
(Garden Zoo)
Av. Las Heras y Av. Sarmiento
Tel.: 4806-7412

Jardín Botánico
(Botanic Garden)
Av. Santa Fe 3951
Tel.: 4832-1552

Jardín Japonés
(Japanesse Garden)
Av. Casares y Av. Adolfo Berro
Tel.: 4804-4922/9141

Paseo del Rosedal
The Roses Garden
Parque Tres de Febrero-
Av. Del Libertador y
Paseo de la infanta

Planetario "Galileo Galilei"
"Galileo Galilei" Observatory
Av. Sarmiento y Roldán
Tel.: 4771-6629/4772-9265